The Mountains of England & Wales
Vol. 1: WALES

Pen yr Helgi Du

The Mountains of England and Wales
Vol.1: WALES

by
John and Anne Nuttall

*Maps and Drawings
by John Nuttall*

CICERONE

© John and Anne Nuttall 1989
Reprinted 1991, 1994

Seconnd edition 1999
ISBN 10: 1 85284 304 7

Third edition 2009
ISBN 13: 978 1 85284 594 0

Acknowledgements

We are grateful for the help given by the staff of the Ordnance Survey who answered our many queries and especially to Peter Opie-Smith for his advice which enabled us to accurately survey the marginal summits. Our thanks also go to Sheila Grigg for her help with the translation of Welsh place names. Finally thank you to our sons Jeremy and Joe who have had to be very self sufficient over the last year and to Joe who programmed the computer to produce lists of maps for checking at the library and to sort the list of mountains into alphabetical order.

Second Edition
Our thanks go to Chartech for the latest waterproof OS maps. Also thanks to all the people who have told us of changes that have taken place on the Welsh mountains over the last ten years, and especially to Dewi Jones and Myrddyn Phillips for discovering the new tops.

Third Edition
Thank you to John Barnard and Graham Jackson for their meticulous surveying work and the help of Leica Geosystems.

Get the latest information from www.nuttalls.com

Other Cicerone books by the same authors:

The Mountains of England and Wales Vol. 2: England
The Tarns of Lakeland Vol. 1: West
The Tarns of Lakeland Vol. 2: East
Walking round The Lakes
Weekend Walks in the Peak District

Front cover: Tryfan
Back cover: Mynydd Drws-y-coed, the start of the Nantlle Ridge

CONTENTS

Pen Llithrig-y-Wrâch from Llyn Cowlyd

INTRODUCTION

The ascent of all the mountains of England and Wales is not an objective one starts out with; it comes rather as the goal of a task already partly achieved after much time spent among the hills. For us it was after many visits to the Lake District and many hundreds of days spent climbing the mountains that we found ourselves within sight of completing all the Wainwrights, that is all the summits described in those seven delightful guides to the Lake District. The achievement of this took us to the less frequented areas where we discovered many fascinating places starting a new chapter in our enjoyment of the hills. What was to be our next objective? We would certainly return and climb again many of the mountains thus discovered and we had also acquired a new approach to the hills by wild camping among them. Sunrise, sunset and the stars at night added new experiences and enjoyment, but we needed a fresh challenge. What was it to be? Well, what about all the rest of the mountains?

The Munros were an obvious choice and one we were soon planning holidays to tackle, but journeys north required several days to produce results and while our present tally has crept up, recently reaching one hundred, an objective closer to home was needed. Thus we came to climb the mountains of England and Wales, but this has been by no means second best. While the grandeur and remoteness of the Scottish hills is on a larger scale, there is so much wild and beautiful mountain country to explore south of the border that one could visit a different place every weekend for years.

Steadily we progressed towards our goal; first the final summit in Snowdonia, then the Brecon Beacons and finally the last Welsh top above the sleepy village of New Radnor. England too was coming on nicely, but we were beginning to get uneasy. The list from which we were working was looking out of date. We were finding unlisted summits and others, resolutely attained after miles of flogging across bog and heather, turned out to hardly merit attention, rising by only trivial amounts above their surroundings.

What was needed, we decided, was an up to date accurate list. Many hours were spent in Manchester Central Reference Library poring over the 1:10,000 maps. A great deal more time was spent in all weathers re-visiting all the tops, and several new ones besides, and in devising ways to link groups of summits into interesting walks.

The year in which we set out on our task proved to be the wettest since records began. What is surprising therefore is that we had a clear view from all but a tiny handful of tops. In fact the only summits from which the cloud has never lifted for us are Arenig Fach and Moel Eilio. On all the others we have been favoured on at least one visit with a complete, if rather grey, panorama. Much of the time we have walked alone with no other person for miles; there is still plenty of room in the hills.

Of the many memorable days we would pick a few to treasure; a brilliantly clear day of ice and snow in the Arans, the fences sparkling with frost needles and long icicles cascading over the rim of the streams; a scorching hot shirtless day above Blaenau Ffestiniog with the evening in the hotel garden, the village looking quite alpine with geranium-filled window boxes; the mist playing hide and seek with the summit rocks of Glyder Fach and the Castle of the Winds, and many nights in our mountain tent high among the hills, while even on days of torrential, unceasing rain there is a wet satisfaction in wading through the rivers and bogs, but all these days have had something special even if it has only been the cold wind in our faces and the freedom of being away among the hills.

It is with sadness that for the coming months we shall no longer be setting off for Wales at the weekends, but instead the mountains of England beckon and there is much to look forward to. We have had a superb year with unforgettable days in the hills. This book is our way of saying thank you and passing on some of our appreciation.

NOTES

There are 190 mountain summits in Wales which reach the height of 2000ft. This book describes how to ascend them all in a series of 49 walks. By completing all the walks the reader will ascend all the Welsh two thousanders.

SELECTION OF THE TOPS

Over the years several lists have been compiled of the Welsh and English mountains. Various criteria for selection have been adopted, but although there seems to be common agreement about the height, 2000ft being universally accepted as the height of a mountain, there has been little consistency about anything else.

Some fanatics have determined to visit every separate ring contour of 2000ft. While relatively easy in the high hills, it must be a boring task among the undulating moors of north-east England and the heather-clad Berwyn Hills where the multiplicity of such separate rings makes nonsense of their claim to be tops. Buxton & Lewis selected only tops with two or more concentric contours, but this has the anomaly that some tops are omitted which actually rise above their surroundings by a greater amount than others which are included.

During the 1970s the Ordnance Survey undertook a complete re-survey of Great Britain using a process of photogrammetry from aerial photographs. The contour interval chosen for this new survey was 10m. The publication of the new maps, known as the second series, is now complete. The most commonly available maps are the 1:50,000 scale (Landranger) and 1:25,000 (Outdoor Leisure and Explorer series). The old Pathfinder series has been replaced by the Explorer maps.

The impact of this new survey has been quite dramatic on the old lists. Many official heights have changed, several tops have proved to lack the necessary rise to merit inclusion, while other brand new tops have been discovered. The collector of single ring contours will find the greatest change in undulating terrain where a few feet more or less creates and deletes tops with gay abandon.

After careful consideration the definition of a mountain adopted for this book is any summit of 2000ft or more which rises above its surroundings on all sides by at least 50ft. Using metric maps this has been refined to 610m and 15m. This choice was based on three factors. Firstly Bridge's Tables, now dethroned by the new survey, used these criteria, secondly to choose more than 15m eliminated too many tops generally considered as separate mountains, and thirdly to choose less than 15m meant including an excessive number of unnamed minor bumps which were unworthy of elevation to mountain status.

No attempt has been made to differentiate between mountains and subsidiary tops. The word 'top' has however been used to denote a summit which has no accepted name on the OS maps. Rather than referring to them as nameless summits, they have been named by reference to a nearby summit or other feature; eg Arenig Fawr South Top.

The vast majority of the tops listed in this book can easily be seen to merit inclusion. The rest can mostly be proved from the contours and spot heights of the new survey, but in a few instances, where no absolute data is available, the case has been decided by personal on the spot surveying using a technique recommended to us by the Ordnance Survey.

It is interesting to note that the spot heights given on the present 1:50,000 maps are derived from the old survey rather than the new, although the contour information itself is the latest. As a result there is sometimes a discrepancy between spot heights given on the 1:50,000 and 1:25,000 maps. In such cases the spot heights from the 1:25,000 and/or the base map at 1:10,000 scale have been used. At the end of the book will be found a list of deleted tops which may be of interest to people already hooked on the game. Game it certainly is, but any game worth playing has rules and we have done our best to provide the reader with as definitive a list as possible.

MAPS

The maps in this book are drawn at a scale of 1:50,000. They are to enable the reader to locate the walk on the relevant OS map and should be used to supplement the OS maps, not replace them.

The best maps for walkers are the 1:25,000 Explorer series and the Outdoor Leisure which between them cover all the mountains of Wales. While it is possible to manage with the 1:50,000 Landranger maps for all the walks in this book, the larger scale, which shows walls, fences and in general much more detail, is highly recommended.

The spelling of place names has been taken throughout from the latest OS maps. Note however that not all names referred to in the text will necessarily be found on the 1:50,000 series. It is interesting to note that the spelling of many Welsh place names has changed significantly in recent years and sometimes maps differ in the spellings of certain words.

The start of each walk is marked 'S' on the map and while every effort has been made to keep north at the top, which is how most people like it, in a few cases this rule has had to be broken. For clarity the route has been marked with a dashed line, but this does not always indicate the presence of a footpath, merely the suggested way.

ACCESS

The Countryside and Rights of Way (CROW) Act 2000 introduced a new right of public access on foot to open country and registered common land in Wales. All the Welsh Mountain summits are on this Open Access land. Sometimes this is reached by public rights of way and just occasionally by routes in general use by hillwalkers.

NEW TOPS

It all started with Dewi Jones, whom we met while we were backpacking on the Brecon Beacons. "You've missed one" he told us. That was Cnicht North Top, but it was Myrddyn Phillips who, not content with multiple rounds of all the tops, managed to find several more. So far Myrddyn has completed 16 rounds. In March 2003 he held a party on Snowdon summit to celebrate climbing every Welsh mountain in each month of the year.

More recently John Barnard and Graham Jackson have been checking our surveys using a Leica Automatic Level and sadly have demoted Cadair Bronwen North East Top. Our apologies to all those completers who needn't have bothered climbing it! Also due to their surveying we have added Castell y Gwynt, the very marginal Carnedd y Filiast North Top and, with Leica Geosystems, Mynydd Graig Goch. Any future changes and the latest news on the mountains will be posted at www.nuttalls.com.

Ffynnon Caseg

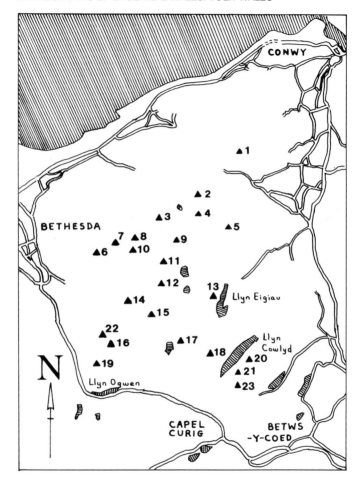

1. THE CARNEDDAU

CHAPTER 1: THE CARNEDDAU

TOP	NAME	HEIGHT	GRID REF	WALK No.
1	Tal y Fan	610m	115-729726 SH	1.3
2	Carnedd y Ddelw	688m	115-708705 SH	1.3
3	Llwytmor	849m	115-689693 SH	1.2
4	Drum	770m	115-708696 SH	1.3
5	Pen y Castell	623m	115-724689 SH	1.3
6	Gyrn Wigau	643m	115-654675 SH	1.2
7	Drosgl	758m	115-664680 SH	1.2
8	Bera Mawr	794m	115-675683 SH	1.2
9	Foel-fras	942m	115-696682 SH	1.2
10	Bera Bach	807m	115-672677 SH	1.2
11	Garnedd Uchaf	926m	115-687669 SH	1.2
12	Foel Grach	976m	115-689659 SH	1.2
13	Craig Eigiau	735m	115-713654 SH	1.4
14	Yr Elen	962m	115-674651 SH	1.1
15	Carnedd Llewelyn	1064m	115-684645 SH	1.1
16	Carnedd Dafydd	1044m	115-663630 SH	1.1
17	Pen yr Helgi Du	833m	115-698630 SH	1.1
18	Pen Llithrig-y-wrâch	799m	115-716623 SH	1.4
19	Pen yr Ole Wen	978m	115-655619 SH	1.1
20	Creigiau Gleision North Top	634m	115-734622 SH	1.4
21	Creigiau Gleision	678m	115-729615 SH	1.4
22	Foel Meirch	800m	115-659637 SH	1.1
23	Craiglwyn	623m	115-731609 SH	1.4

WALK 1.1   CARNEDD LLEWELYN AND THE WESTERN CARNEDDAU

SUMMITS:	Pen yr Ole Wen	3209ft (978m)
	Carnedd Dafydd	3425ft (1044m)
	Foel Meirch	2625ft (800m)
	Yr Elen	3156ft (962m)
	Carnedd Llewelyn	3491ft (1064m)
	Pen yr Helgi Du	2733ft (833m)

DISTANCE: 12 miles

ASCENT: 4200 feet

MAPS: OS Landranger sheet 115
Explorer OL17 - Snowdon / Yr Wyddfa

STARTING
POINT   (115-668605) The east end of Llyn Ogwen, there is ample parking beside the A5.

The Carneddau is the largest area above 3000ft anywhere south of the Scottish Highlands. From Pen yr Ole Wen above the Ogwen valley, a broad high ridge nearly seven miles long runs northwards over Carnedd Llewelyn and then gradually descends to terminate in the lowly outpost of Tal y Fan which just reaches 2000ft.

No side turnings distract the traffic on the busy A5 to the south and while from the Conwy valley narrow winding country lanes penetrate a short way into the mountains, no major roads intrude and this vast upland area of around 70 square miles is wild and splendidly remote.

Carnedd Llewelyn, the third highest mountain in Wales, has long been a popular ascent, though nowhere near a rival to Snowdon or Tryfan. Now even the northern and eastern Carneddau are increasing in popularity, but although more people are discovering the attractions of these hills, it is still an area where often one has only the ravens for company.

The small attractive mountain lakes in the southern Carneddau are all called Ffynnon, that is spring or well. Here is Ffynnon Caseg, the mare's well and one of the loveliest, where according to tradition, the wild ponies come each year to foal beneath the cliffs of Yr Elen. Close under the eastern slopes of Carnedd Llewelyn is Ffynnon Llyffant, the frog's well, while high on the side of Pen yr Ole Wen is Ffynnon Lloer, the spring of the moon. Ffynnon Llugwy, the well of clear water and the largest of them all, is appropriately named for it is used as a reservoir as are the larger lakes on the eastern side of the hills.

The origin of the names of Carnedd Llewelyn and Carnedd Dafydd is

14

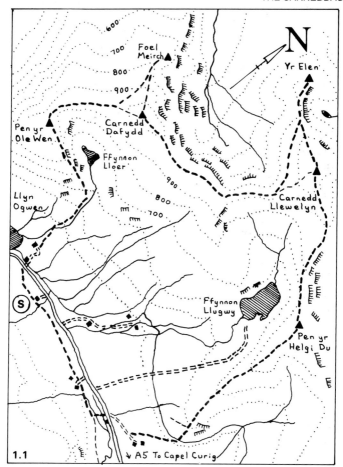

1.1

unclear. They were probably named either after Llewelyn the Great (1194-1240) who had a fortified observation post on the mountain and his successor David, or the two last Welsh princes Llewelyn ap Gruffydd and his brother David.

The 2000ft south ridge of Pen yr Ole Wen, which drops precipitously to the west end of Llyn Ogwen, is an unremitting and undeviating climb straight

15

treacherously loose ascent. Fortunately there is a less obvious, but very much more attractive approach by way of Cwm Lloer and the mountain's eastern ridge. It is surprising that this route is so little used that the path is in places quite indistinct.

ROUTE DESCRIPTION

PEN YR OLE WEN *(Head of the White Slope)*

Take the footpath leading north by Glan Dena which belongs to the Midland Association of Mountaineers. A ladder stile crosses the wall above Tal y Llyn Ogwen Farm and after crossing the Afon Lloer this is followed on an indistinct path to a second ladder stile. From here the route lies up the east ridge which appears at first sight to be a difficult ascent of steep rocks, but an improving path neatly picks its way through the rocky obstacles with only a short and easy section of scrambling, to emerge above the barrier high above Ffynnon Lloer. The whole ascent is delightful with Tryfan towering dramatically above Llyn Ogwen to the left. The path continues to the summit of Pen yr Ole Wen, which is flat and stony with a rough cairn on the highest point, commanding good views of the surrounding mountains. Tryfan is still the centre-piece though now much diminished with the Glyders behind. Bethesda and Anglesey lie to the north-west, ahead are Carnedd Dafydd and Carnedd Llewelyn, while to the east is Pen Llithrig-y-wrâch and the distant Creigiau Gleision.

FOEL MEIRCH *(Hill of the Stallion)*

Follow the main path north along the ridge, which is at first carpeted with the red cowberry, for nearly a mile, passing a couple of ancient cairns. As you make the final ascent to the summit of Carnedd Dafydd a detour north-west is necessary to include the top of Foel Meirch. It feels a long way down, but you can blame the enthusiasm of Myrddyn Phillips who discovered the top in 1997.

CARNEDD DAFYDD *(David's Cairn)*

You now have to retrace your steps back up to the ridge - it's only 800ft! The ancient cairn on the summit of Carnedd Dafydd has been refashioned to form a series of windbreaks and a small cairn. Yr Elen the next objective now comes into view and the route to Carnedd Llewelyn with the dramatic cliffs of Ysgolion Duon, the black ladders, at the head of the deserted Cwm Pen-llafar. This is a climbers' cliff, the 900ft Western Gully was first ascended in 1901.

YR ELEN *(The Hill of the Fawn)*

Follow the ridge east for about a mile and a half of dramatic walking. To the left is a precipitous drop over the sheer cliffs of Ysgolion Duon while to the right are grassy slopes; the worst rough bouldery sections can easily be avoided by descending a little to the right. The ridge switchbacks along, finishing with a narrow pointed stony section before the slopes of Carnedd Llewelyn are joined at a col where the ground flattens out and becomes grassy. In misty conditions head north-west, climbing gradually to join the ridge from Carnedd Llewelyn to Yr Elen. In good visibility aim to the right of the lowest rocky tor on the skyline passing many little springs where the starry saxifrage can be found. From the rock outcrop a little path descends gently through the scree to the col, where you can see the rocky tops of Bera Bach and Bera Mawr with the sea beyond. A good path is followed north-west along the edge of the rocky cwm, high above Ffynnon Caseg, to the summit of Yr Elen. A little cairn crowns the highest rocky point and the further cairn should be visited for more extensive views over towards the sea.

CARNEDD LLEWELYN *(Llewelyn's Cairn)*
Retrace you steps to the col, then continue along the edge of Cwm Caseg on a good path, climbing up to the right after about half a mile to the summit of Carnedd Llewelyn, crowned with its ancient cairn. The top is very flat, with the most central cairn taken to be the highest point; the windshelter is a little nearer to the edge. From here you can look down into Cwm Eigiau and there are extensive views of the rest of the Carneddau range and the Glyders.

PEN YR HELGI DU *(Head of the Black Hound)*
A cairn marks the start of the good path east which leads high above the rocky cwm containing Ffynnon Llyffant to descend gradually, in about a mile, to the rocky knob of Craig yr Ysfa, crag of the sheepwalk. If you look down towards Amphitheatre Wall you can see the Pinnacle which was first climbed solo in 1931 by Colin Kirkus. A dramatic narrow rocky ridge leads from here first down to the col and then steeply up to the flat grassy summit of Pen yr Helgi Du. There is a bird's-eye view of the ruined quarries in Cwm Eigiau below to the left and Ffynnon Llugwy Reservoir to the right. A small cairn at the end of the ridge marks the highest point and there are extensive views towards Llandudno and Conwy Bay.

Leaving the next summit, Pen Llithrig-y-wrâch, for another day, descend gradually south along a faint grassy path for about a mile to a wall. The path bends sharply right here but continue downhill in the same direction to cross a stile by the leat. An indistinct path slants down across the field to a ladder stile to join the farm track and this is followed to the A5. On the opposite side of the road a footpath crosses the river to join the track which follows the line of the old Holyhead road, which was constructed at the end of the eighteenth century by Lord Penrhyn. This is a much pleasanter walk back to the starting point than using Telford's busy new road.

WALK 1.2 THE CENTRAL CARNEDDAU

SUMMITS:	Llwytmor	2785ft (849m)
	Foel-fras	3091ft (942m)
	Garnedd Uchaf	3038ft (926m)
	Foel Grach	3202ft (976m)
	Bera Mawr	2605ft (794m)
	Bera Bach	2648ft (807m)
	Drosgl	2487ft (758m)
	Gyrn Wigau	2110ft (643m)

DISTANCE: 12¹/₂ miles

ASCENT: 3750 feet

MAPS: OS Landranger sheet 115
Explorer OL17 - Snowdon / Yr Wyddfa

STARTING
POINT: (115-664719) Forestry Commission car park 1 mile south-east of Aber village, small fee, toilets.

The northern slopes of the Carneddau offer a complete contrast to the more frequented southern approaches. Here smooth grassy slopes sweep down towards the sea incised by long valleys where Aber Falls attracts the crowds, but other valleys are wild and deserted. Once up, the walking on the long ridge is easy underfoot with interest maintained by a succession of rocky tops.

In cloud the area is a challenge to navigation with few landmarks on the extensive plateau and the difficulty of escape in bad weather makes the Carneddau a more serious proposition than many of the mountains of Snowdonia. It is very easy to descend into the wrong valley or mistake where you are, as we found after a very chilly picnic on the summit of Foel Grach, only a stone's throw from the relative comfort of the Mountain Refuge. After an ascent from Cwm Eigiau and thinking we were on Garnedd Uchaf, it was with considerable surprise that we saw the upright stones which cross the ridge and point the way to the hut. This refuge was erected by the Mountaineering Club of North Wales and Caernarfonshire County Council and for 25 years has withstood the seasons. It is a sturdily built stone construction and on all of our visits it has been a pleasant surprise to find it clean and tidy. Approaching the hut on a backpacking trip at Christmas 1988, we were saddened to find the roof gone and a temporary tin hut skulking within the walls. However the refuge has since been rebuilt.

Aber was once the home of Llewelyn the Great, the most powerful of the Welsh princes, who died in 1240. It is a long walk from this pretty little village

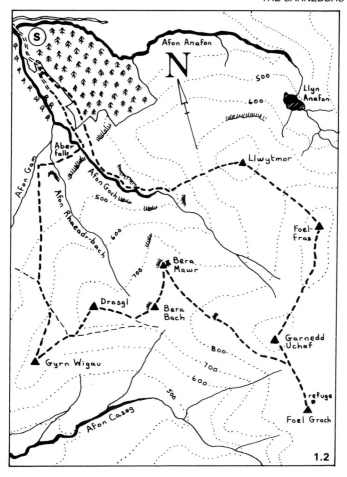

to gain the high plateau, but the lower slopes are pastoral and most attractive with a truly magnificent waterfall. The walk climbs right above the falls and follows the delightful little river up into a secluded valley with a final steep climb, but nowhere difficult, to reach Llwytmor, the first summit.

Aber Falls, Rhaeadr-fawr, which translated just means big waterfall, is

19

Yr Elen from Bera Bach

indeed big. The Afon Goch falls for more than 100ft over the cliffs which are composed of a band of granophyre, a hard igneous rock only rarely found in Snowdonia, over which the stream tumbles, cutting into the softer shales below.

ROUTE DESCRIPTION

LLWYTMOR *(Big Grey Hill)*

From the Forest Commission car park, whose grassy banks are studded with primroses in the spring, walk back to the river and turn left to follow the track on the east side of the Afon Rhaeadr-fawr, through the nature reserve. A strange roaring sound comes from wind in the electricity cables strung high on pylons across the valley; an unfortunate contrast to the beauty of the valley and the ancient oaks beneath. The trees to the left of the path are estimated to be about 220 years old. Taking the left fork at the trial enclosures just before Nant cottage, the path leads beside the wood and gives a good view of the waterfall with Bera Mawr above. Enter the wood at a stile and climb gently uphill to emerge onto the open hillside on the edge of the screes close to the waterfall.

After crossing the screes, a delightful little path climbs up into the valley above, along rocky ledges above the falls. Follow the east bank of the Afon

Goch for about a mile on a faint path, past the large sheepfolds, to where the rocky ridge of Bera Mawr runs down to join the stream by a series of pretty falls. From here head east climbing steeply over grass, bedecked in spring with wood sorrel and violets, to follow a grassy rake which leads left of the jagged cliffs, all the way to the top. A rocky tor with a huge hollowed-out cairn beside it stands out dramatically, but the highest point is a few yards further on over grass where the flat, stony top is marked with a cairn. The view ahead is limited by the Carneddau ridge, but to the right can be seen Bera Mawr, Bera Bach, and Drosgl.

FOEL-FRAS *(Prominent Bare Hill)*
It is about a mile to the next summit. A simple descent south-east over a peaty col and an easy climb of about 500ft over grass leads to the highest point, an OS trig point by a sturdy stone wall on a rough bouldery top.

GARNEDD UCHAF *(Highest Cairn)*
The wall sets off south-west towards the next top, with the rest of the Carneddau range ahead. Where it changes to a fence, the path veers away right over grass, and marked by upright stones heads towards the stony summit. The highest point is a rocky tor to the right of the path from which there are good views back to Llwytmor and ahead to the higher Carneddau.

FOEL GRACH *(Scabby Bare Hill)*
The path continues easily over grass and then climbs to the Foel Grach Refuge below the summit, which can be located in bad weather by a line of standing stones crossing the ridge at this point. The summit is a little higher up with a small hollowed-out cairn on top. Carnedd Llewelyn looks temptingly close with Yr Elen to the right.

BERA MAWR *(Great Hayricks)*
Retrace your steps to the col and fork left on an indistinct path, which marked with standing stones, leads round beneath the tumbled rocks of Garnedd Uchaf. Head north-west to the left of the rocky knoll Yr Aryg picking the best route over the boulders and continue in the same direction over grass to the magnificent rocky outcrop of Bera Mawr ahead. Scramble up to the left, past a rocky platform with a perched boulder, then pass between two massive monoliths reminiscent of Adam and Eve on Tryfan. The final rocks offer a last challenge and an easy ascent can be made on the north side.

BERA BACH *(Little Hayricks)*
Descend by the same route, then walk over grass aiming to the left of Bera Bach, which though less impressive than its twin and despite its name is in fact higher. An easy scramble leads to the unmarked top.

DROSGL *(Rough Ground)*
Head south from the summit to pick up the main path which leads to the south of Drosgl. At the col take an indistinct path which makes a beeline for the stony top. The highest point is marked by a cairn and there is a huge hollowed-out ancient cairn a little to the north.

GYRN WIGAU *(Wooded Peak)*
The last top is about a mile south-west with a stony descent at first. Aim directly for the summit crossing the main path at the broad col. A gentle stroll over grass leads to a little grassy ridge with pointed rocks, giving the impression of a slumbering dinosaur. The unmarked top is in the centre of the ridge, just 50ft above the lowest point at the col.

Follow the ridge north-east and contour along the grassy slope to pick up the good track which descends to the col south of Moel Wnion. To the left is the rocky little summit of Gyrn, which has a complicated array of sheepfolds on its east flank. Head north-east back to Aber, keeping high above the Afon Gam where the going is easier and descend to cross the fence at the bottom, over a step stile, to enter the nature reserve. Turn right and follow the footpath by drifts of bluebells beneath Rhaeadr-bach, a beautiful waterfall which would be famous if it were situated anywhere else. At the foot of Rhaeadr-fawr, cross the Afon Rhaeadr-fawr and take the main track back beside the river to your starting point.

Maen y Bardd

WALK 1.3 THE NORTHERN CARNEDDAU

SUMMITS:	Tal y Fan	2001ft (610m)
	Carnedd y Ddelw	2257ft (688m)
	Drum	2526ft (770m)
	Pen y Castell	2044ft (623m)
DISTANCE:	10 miles	
ASCENT:	2750 feet	
MAPS:	OS Landranger sheet 115	
	Explorer OL17 - Snowdon / Yr Wyddfa	
STARTING		
POINT:	(115-731714) On the minor road leading from the Conwy valley to the south of Tal y Fan. A few cars may be parked on the verge and there is a car park half a mile further up the road.	

The whole of the northern Carneddau is scattered with relics of Bronze Age and Iron Age occupation with standing stones, hut circles and burial chambers. Tal y Fan, the most northerly outpost of the Carneddau is separated from the rest of the mountain range by Bwlch y Ddeufaen, pass of the two stones, and the two huge prehistoric stones which give the pass its name still survive, standing prominently one on either side of the track at the head of the pass. The way was used by the Romans as a principal route to Caernarfon and was sufficiently important to warrant milestones. The lane to the youth hostel, which is part of the Roman road, passes Maen y Bardd, the Bard's stone, a splendid example of a cromlech or burial chamber built by megalithic man while Graiglwyd, to the east of the Penmaenmawr quarries, on the north slopes of Tal y Fan, is the site of a neolithic stone axe factory.

Of all the wealth of antiquities hidden in these hills, the most famous is Pen-y-gaer, an impressive Iron Age hill fort. On the east side of the fort the ground drops steeply away, but the rest of the hill is defended by two concentric ramparts, one of stone and one of earth, while inside the fortifications are traces of hut circles. It is the only hill fort In England and Wales to possess chevaux de frise. These are sharply pointed stones set vertically into the ground to repel invaders, a sort of Iron Age Maginot Line. Other examples of this type occur mainly in western Ireland.

Exploring Pen-y-gaer one very hot afternoon and expecting to see stones several feet high protruding from the grass, we arrived at the top of the hill disappointed. Another couple were sitting by the cairn proclaiming they had come to the wrong spot and had failed to find the famous stones. Reassuring them that they were in the right place, we joined forces to form a search party composed of two men, two women and one dog. This more thorough search

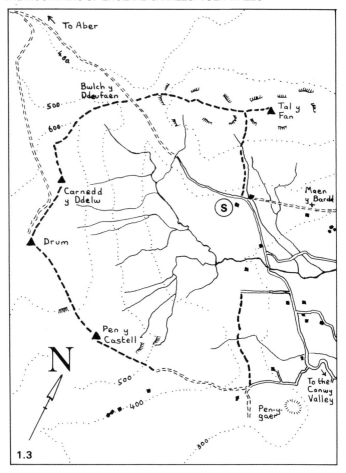

1.3

revealed several examples to the west and south-west well down the slope. They are large groups of small stones, set on end protruding a foot or so from the ground and would have very effectively slowed up attacking invaders. Pausing to greet a charming elderly Welshman we mentioned our recent difficulties, "I've been looking for the buggers all afternoon," he exclaimed, "They're over there," pointing with his stick to another little group.

ROUTE DESCRIPTION

TAL Y FAN *(End Peak)*

A ladder stile from the lane leads to the right of way which climbs gently uphill through gorse bushes and grassy fields to the left of Cae Coch farmhouse. The waymarked path leads straight up to the col where a final ladder stile is crossed and the west side of the wall followed to the rocky summit, which just scrapes the magic 2000ft height. An OS trig point stands on the other side of the wall by a stile, commanding a superb view for such a modest altitude. Anglesey, Conwy Bay, Llandudno and the Vale of Conwy lie spread out beneath this the most northerly of the Welsh mountains.

CARNEDD Y DDELW *(Cairn of the Idol)*

Retrace your steps and continue to follow the path beside the wall over a lesser summit to the line of pylons at Bwlch y Ddeufaen, pass of the two stones. The stones can clearly be seen standing one on each side of the old Roman road, a little to the east. A stiff pull up of nearly 1000ft on grass, first beside a wall and then a fence, leads to the summit where the ancient cairn has been hollowed-out, forming a shelter. A small golden figure was found here when the cairn was excavated in the eighteenth century. From here to the south-west you can see Llyn Anafon, which supplies water to Llanfairfechan, with Llwytmor above.

DRUM *(Ridge)*

A gentle descent south beside the fence to the wide col and then an easy ascent over grass, leads in half a mile to another ancient cairn, Carnedd Penydorth-goch, on the round grassy top of Drum. This large cairn has been made into a substantial shelter with a level floor. Foel-fras looms ahead with the summit rocks of Bera Mawr peeping over the Llwytmor col, while to the west lies the village of Aber.

PEN Y CASTELL *(Top of the Castle)*

The main ridge of the Carneddau is now forsaken to descend towards the Conwy valley over the final outlying top of Pen y Castell. A fence leads east over the broad grassy ridge passing a collection of sheepfolds below Foel L Lŵyd. To the south-west are the black cliffs of Craig y Dulyn with Melynllyn glimpsed beyond. After three-quarters of a mile, a short climb leads to the attractive rock-studded top of heather and bilberry, the highest point being a rocky tor at the far end. To the left, a rocky outcrop has been decorated with upright stones, giving a weird impression of modern sculpture. There is a wide panorama from the summit with the whole route of the walk displayed.

Continue along the ridge towards Penygadair, turning right at the stone wall before the col. Descend to the right of way, an old road, which is followed east. This crosses a leat which fed the now empty Llyn Eigiau Reservoir. At the lane cross the ladder stile opposite to visit Pen-y-gaer hill fort and then return the same way over the fields to the lane. Just below the junction of the two lanes cross the left-hand wall at a stone step stile. A ruined wall leads north-west to another stile by a hog hole. Keeping to the left of the contouring wall, cross two more descending walls by sturdy stiles, then follow the edge of the field round to the right to join the end of an old road at a gate near a ruined building. This leads downhill to join a very minor road. Turn left and from here it is just over a mile back along this quiet little country lane to the start of the walk.

WALK 1.4 THE EASTERN CARNEDDAU

SUMMITS:	Craig Eigiau	2411ft (735m)
	Pen Llithrig-y-wrâch	2621ft (799m)
	Craiglwyn	2044ft (623m)
	Creigiau Gleision	2224ft (678m)
	Creigiau Gleision North Top	2080ft (634m)
DISTANCE:	11½ miles	
ASCENT:	3560 feet	
MAPS:	OS Landranger sheet 115	
	Explorer OL17 - Snowdon / Yr Wyddfa	
STARTING POINT:	(115-732663) The end of the surfaced road 3 miles south-west of Tal-y-Bont. Small car park.	

Cwm Eigiau and the eastern Carneddau have long been among the quieter parts of Snowdonia although the area is increasing in popularity (there is even a small car park now at the end of the road from the Conwy valley into this remote cwm). Nevertheless it is still a place to be alone, where another walker is the exception, rather than the rule.

This air of remoteness, peace and tranquillity is only one phase of the area's history. The slopes below Llyn Dulyn show evidence of Bronze Age settlement. In those times the weather would have been warmer and drier and the name of the valley, Pant y Griafolen, rowan tree hollow, speaks of sunnier days. There are traces of cairns, hut circles, walled enclosures and terraced fields.

The quarry at the head of Cwm Eigiau closed in 1870 and although it seems a very remote place in which to live and work, the valley at that time would have had many working farms. We spent a wet Sunday morning here while backpacking round the Carneddau. The only people we met were a large group of young people in the charge of a harassed-looking man who was

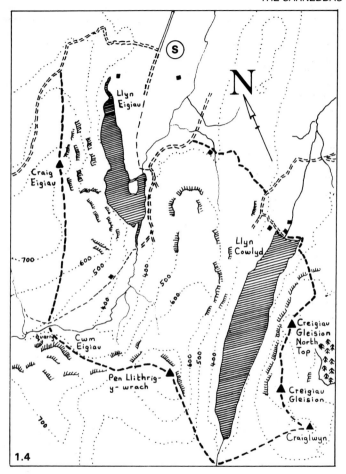

1.4

totally lost. They were due to be met in Ogwen in half an hour and were relieved to learn that Bwlch Trimarchog could be crossed, as the cliffs appear continuous around the cwm from below.

On another backpacking holiday at Easter in 1984, we encountered a huge fire which was raging over the Creigiau Gleision area, indeed we were forced to retreat to the other side of the A5 where we watched with horror the flames leaping high into the sky as darkness fell. A year later the ground was still blackened, but the vegetation had started to regenerate and in 1988 only a few bare patches still remained.

Llyn Eigiau was the scene of a terrible disaster in 1923. The dam was breached and a wall of water rushed down into the valley, destroying the aluminium works and a row of cottages in Dolgarrog, killing 16 people. The dam was never repaired and the reservoir, much diminished, now only supplies water by tunnel to Llyn Cowlyd. A complicated system of leats supplies both these reservoirs with water and a massive pipeline carries the water from Llyn Cowlyd into the Conwy valley to supply the large aluminium works with hydroelectric power and also Colwyn Bay with water. The tall dam wall now stands high and dry above the lake.

The twin lakes of Dulyn and Melynllyn which can be glimpsed on the ascent of Craig Eigiau are also reservoirs and send water to Llandudno. Many aircraft were lost in this area during the war and their sad remains can be found scattered around this part of the Carneddau.

ROUTE DESCRIPTION

CRAIG EIGIAU *(Shoal of Fish Rock)*
From the car park at the end of the lane, go through the gate and follow the rough track which leads north-west, crossing the wide valley and then climbing round the north end of the Craig Eigiau ridge. After about a mile cross a ladder stile and climb left over easy grass to follow the wall along the ridge. Just beyond a perched boulder Llyn Dulyn comes into view. The far side of the wall is rough heather, but this side the grass is short and the walking easy. The wall becomes a fence which leads up to the long rocky rib of the summit. The highest point is at the far end of the glacier-smoothed rocks. The whole area is most attractive and you will be tempted to linger here, scrambling around exploring the rocks. No cairn is necessary to mark the highest point and surrounded by the high Carneddau you can look down upon Llyn Eigiau in the valley below.

PEN LLITHRIG-Y-WRÂCH *(Slippery Hill of the Witch)*
Descend south-west over grassy slopes into the head of Cwm Eigiau, heading straight for Pen yr Helgi Du, with the dramatic cliffs of Craig yr Ysfa ahead. Cross the Afon Eigiau by the ruined quarries, to pick up a little path which runs from beside the slate spoil tips round to below Bwlch Trimarchog, pass of the three horsemen. Higher up in the quarry is a tiny hut, still in good condition, that provides shelter in bad weather. This path is little more than a sheep track, but it takes you well on the way until finally giving up in a bouldery area, only to reappear again below the bwlch. Scramble up to the ridge just to the right of the rocky rib above an enclosure in Cwm Eigiau; the adjacent gullies are rather awkward and best avoided. The now diminished Llyn Eigiau

with its breached dam can be seen from here.

Turn left along the ridge where a good path climbs the 600ft to the neat summit cairn of Pen Llithrig-y-wrâch. From the grassy top can be seen the whole of the long Carneddau ridge, stretching from Pen yr Ole Wen over Carnedd Llewelyn to Drum and Tal y Fan. To the south-west are the Glyders with Snowdon behind and to the south Moel Siabod. The Conwy valley lies to the east and you can trace the course of the river all the way to the sea at Conwy Bay.

CRAIGLWYN *(Bush Rock)*
To the east the mountain drops precipitously to Llyn Cowlyd, so to descend to Bwlch Cowlyd turn south and follow the edge of the cliffs down the ridge, with Tryfan standing out dramatically across the valley. The intermittent little path leads to a bridge where the leat discharges into the reservoir below.

From the bwlch it is a steady climb east, first over heather and cotton grass, then short turf to the small cairn on this new summit. Craiglwyn was wrongly omitted from the earlier list of tops as the OS spot height on the col is misleadingly not at the lowest point. The survey reveals a rise of 68ft.

CREIGIAU GLEISION *(Blue Rocks)*
Following the ridge north a path leads to the next top. It is a pleasant scramble up the summit rocks to the highest point which is marked with a few stones. To the right is the beautiful Betws-y-Coed forest with its many little lakes and Llyn Crafnant Reservoir, while below on the west side lies Llyn Cowlyd Reservoir.

Eilio near Llyn Eigiau

CREIGIAU GLEISION NORTH TOP

A narrow path winds between the rocky and heathery knolls of the ridge. After passing a startlingly white promontory of quartz high above Llyn Cowlyd, the path climbs to the bilberry-covered rocks of the second top which is crowned with a small pile of stones. It is two miles from here as the crow flies, back to the Llyn Eigiau road with its tiny row of cars.

Continue along the ridge until you meet a fence which can be followed down north. This crosses an area which is very rich botanically, with many more flowers than is usual in Snowdonia, to the boggy and bouldery shores of Llyn Cowlyd Reservoir, which is over 200ft deep. Cross the dam above the pipe line which disappears down the valley, to a large building which offers shelter. Zigzag up the track, turn right at the junction and follow it for about 250 yards along the hillside to some enclosures, the site of Garreg-wen Farm. From here a waymarked footpath leads over the Moel Eilio col and then descends passing by the now empty Eilio Cottage, to join the rough road to Llyn Eigiau. Turn left up to the end of the reservoir and then follow the track past the broken dam wall, back to the starting point. Below the breach in the wall you can clearly see the channel the water scoured out of the ground and the debris left behind when it poured down into the valley below.

Tryfan from Llyn Ogwen

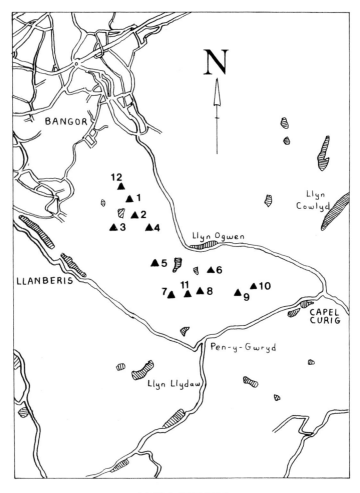

2. THE GLYDERS

CHAPTER 2: THE GLYDERS

TOP	NAME	HEIGHT	GRID REF	WALK No.
1	Carnedd y Filiast	821m	115-620628 SH	2.2
2	Mynydd Perfedd	812m	115-623619 SH	2.2
3	Elidir Fawr	924m	115-612613 SH	2.2
4	Foel-goch	831m	115-629612 SH	2.2
5	Y Garn	947m	115-631596 SH	2.2
6	Tryfan	915m	115-664594 SH	2.3
7	Glyder Fawr	999m	115-642580 SH	2.1
8	Glyder Fach	994m	115-656583 SH	2.1
9	Y Foel Goch	805m	115-678582 SH	2.3
10	Gallt yr Ogof	763m	115-685586 SH	2.3
11	Castell y Gwynt	972m	115-654581 SH	2.1
12	Carnedd y Filiast North Top	721m	115-617631 SH	2.2

Snowdon from Castell y Gwynt

WALK 2.1 THE GLYDERS

SUMMITS:	Glyder Fach	3261ft (994m)
	Castell y Gwynt	3189ft (972m)
	Glyder Fawr	3278ft (999m)

DISTANCE:	5 miles
ASCENT:	2550 feet
MAPS:	OS Landranger sheet 115
	Explorer OL17 - Snowdon / Yr Wyddfa
STARTING POINT:	(115-649604) The west end of Llyn Ogwen on the A5. Car park and toilets.

Between the busy A5 with its almost unbroken line of traffic speeding along this main highway to the west and the twisting road which squeezes its way between the steep rock walls of the Llanberis Pass, lies a group of mountains which are second only to Snowdon itself in popularity. These mountains are indeed among some of the best with rock slabs and walls rising amid grand surroundings to fine summits of naked rock. The Cantilever Stone, looking exactly as it did in the illustration in Pennant's eighteenth-century *Tour in Wales*, Castell y Gwynt, which has now joined the elite as a 3000er, and other jumbled rocks make the summit area a fascinating place, especially in mist when sudden clearings in the swirling cloud play tricks with perspective and the rocks appear gigantic.

Several circuits of the Glyders can be devised, but the approach via Llyn Bochlwyd, returning via the Devil's Kitchen and the Llyn Ogwen Nature Reserve, is one of the best. If possible do the walk in late spring or early summer in order to see the alpine flora for which Cwm Idwal, the first nature reserve in Wales, is justly famous. The flowers are at their best on the steep cliffs and the black chasm of Twll Du, a deep cleft in the rocks down which a stream falls for nearly 1000ft. Most of Snowdonia's rocks are acidic with an inevitably limited variety of species, but on these cliffs layers of igneous and sedimentary rocks include those rich in lime and here a surprisingly large number of plants flourish, including several more usually found in lowland meadows. The arctic-alpine plants, of which there is a wide variety on these cliffs, are a relic of the last Ice Age; discovered first in the seventeenth century, they have been preserved because of their inaccessibility. Although the cwm itself was formed by glacial action leaving behind moraines and other evidence of glaciation, it is only relatively recently that these signs were recognised. Even Charles Darwin, who first visited the cwm in the early nineteenth century, did not recognise the forces at work on his first visit.

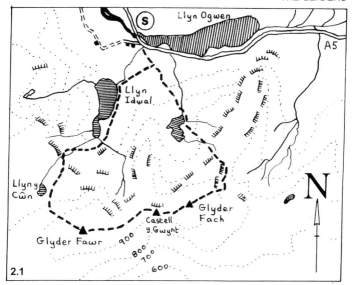

The massive smooth rock of Idwal Slabs, first climbed in 1895, is tilted at an angle just too steep to walk up. Despite the apparently easy slope, the sense of exposure grows with height and it is still very popular with Hope, Faith and Charity being three of its famous routes.

Ogwen itself consists of a youth hostel, café and outdoor pursuits centre. Idwal Cottage, opened in 1931, was one of the first youth hostels in Britain and Ogwen Cottage, the outdoor pursuits centre, was once an inn. The road beside the lake was not built until 1791 and the original packhorse bridge can still be seen under the modern bridge above the falls of Benglog.

ROUTE DESCRIPTION

GLYDER FACH (Small Mound of Stones)

Take the footpath beside Ogwen Cottage to Llyn Idwal and after a quarter of a mile leave this major high road at the bend, continuing in the same direction on an indistinct section. Climb beside the Nant Bochlwyd on a now much-repaired path leading to Llyn Bochlwyd and Bwlch Tryfan. At the bwlch cross the wall at the twin ladder stiles and follow the easy path which zigzags up through the screes to the left of the north-east Bristly Ridge. Joining the east ridge, follow the main cairned path through the jumbled boulders and up past the Cantilever Stone. The summit is 100 yards due west, a huge pile of massive boulders like an enormous cairn thrown up by some giant hand

The Cantilever on Glyder Fach

and the top entails some scrambling to attain it. There are grand views over the surrounding mountain ranges of the Carneddau, Moel Siabod, Snowdon, the rest of the Glyders and down into the Ogwen valley towards the sea.

CASTELL Y GWYNT *(Castle of the Winds)*
The path goes to the left of this new summit which involves an awkward scramble to reach the topmost rocks.

GLYDER FAWR *(Large Mound of Stones)*
A good path leads via Bwlch y Ddwy-Glyder to climb easily to the top of Glyder Fawr. There are two rocky tors of apparently equal height on the flat, bouldery plateau, but the left-hand one is favoured with the spot height.

Continue west along the ridge with its plethora of cairns and descend north-west down one of the many badly eroded paths to Llyn y Cŵn, lake of the dogs. From here a main track leads north-east steeply down under the cliffs of Twll Du, the Devil's Kitchen, to Llyn Idwal. If time permits, a short detour to view the top of the cliffs where the stream plunges over should be included and if the season is right much time can be spent hunting round here and on the cliffs above the path for the alpine flowers for which it is so famous. Walk round the east side of the lake passing beneath Idwal Slabs. From here it is about a mile back along the main path to Ogwen.

WALK 2.2 NORTH OF THE GLYDERS

SUMMITS:	Elidir Fawr	3031ft (924m)
	Mynydd Perfedd	2664ft (812m)
	Carnedd y Filiast	2694ft (821m)
	Carnedd y Filiast North Top	2365ft (721m)
	Foel-goch	2726ft (831m)
	Y Garn	3107ft (947m)

DISTANCE: 9¹/₂ miles

ASCENT: 4350 feet

MAPS: OS Landranger sheet 115
Explorer OL17 - Snowdon / Yr Wyddfa

STARTING
POINT: (115-607583) Nant Peris on the A4086, 2¹/₂ miles east of Llanberis. Car park, toilets.

The area north of the Glyders takes in six summits in a ridge stretching from Llyn y Cŵn, above the Devil's Kitchen at over 2300ft, northwards until it divides to embrace Marchlyn Mawr. The east side of the ridge presents an almost continuously steep and rocky face to the Ogwen valley, while the western slopes drop steeply, though less ruggedly, towards Nant Peris. The area is popular enough, but not as frequented as further east on Tryfan and the Glyders, and underfoot the going is easy until the final steep descent to the valley.

To the north the ridge ends in the horrendous Penrhyn slate quarries. Dating from the fifteenth century this once employed 3500 men and was the largest slate quarry in the world: it is still working. Above Nant Peris stretch the multiple scars of the Dinorwic excavations which employed nearly as many men as the Penrhyn and was worked in galleries or terraces which can clearly be seen. It closed in 1969 but was re-opened as a museum in 1972. Even the heart of the mountain has been torn out in constructing a pumped storage scheme beneath Elidir Fawr. Yet these blemishes can be forgotten for the most part as one strides out with cloud shadows rippling across the hills and one's eyes fixed on a superb panorama of Snowdonia.

The work of the quarrymen is described in the Welsh Slate Centre at the Padarn Country Park, Llanberis and it is well worth a visit. Even the pumped storage scheme has a certain fascination about it, but it is difficult to forgive what has been done to Marchlyn Mawr. There is much to see in Llanberis on a wet day for as well as the Slate Centre and an Information Centre for the Dinorwic Power Station, there is the National Museum of Wales, the Lake Railway and of course the Snowdon Mountain Railway.

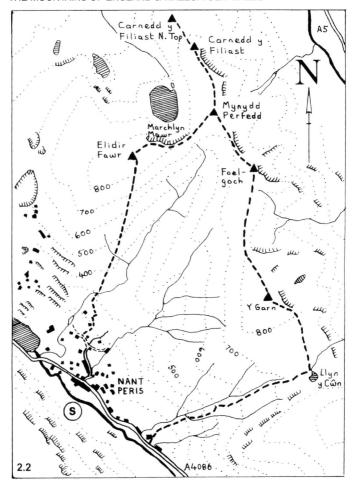

ROUTE DESCRIPTION

ELIDIR FAWR *(Big Elidir)*

Go up the lane beside the chapel, opposite the post office and turn left along the public footpath passing a few houses. After a gate slant upwards across the field, passing a small barn, to a ladder stile in the corner of the field at

Winter on Elidir Fawr

the top. The path shortly gains the open hillside at a gate and zigzags up to follow the stream to a narrow footbridge. Crossing this to the foot of the south-west ridge of Elidir Fawr a steady and unrelenting ascent of over 2000ft lies ahead. A mainly clear path on grass climbs at first straight up to the right of a stream to a ladder stile and then makes a beeline for the rocky summit where there is a windshelter and a cairn.

MYNYDD PERFEDD *(Middle Mountain)*
Descending eastwards along the narrow ridge from the summit of Elidir Fawr watch for the start of the ascent to Mynydd Perfedd at Bwlch y Marchlyn, as the obvious path hurries you off to Foel-goch. The flat, stony top with a cairn and a circular stone windshelter is easily gained and although you will pass this way again in a few minutes after visiting Carnedd y Filiast, there's no rule that says you can't visit a mountain twice in one day! From here there are good views of the Carneddau and the rest of the Glyder range.

CARNEDD Y FILIAST *(Cairn of the Greyhound)*
Ten minutes easy walking northwards brings you to a ladder stile over a wall and, just beyond, the northern outpost of the Glyders is reached. A cairn denotes the highest point and 25 yards away and slightly lower is a windshelter, which is the better viewpoint out to Anglesey. To the south-west you can see Elidir Fawr above Marchlyn Mawr Reservoir.

39

CARNEDD Y FILIAST NORTH TOP

To collect this new top involves an out and back to a rather boring grassy topped bump, but blame John and Graham for the extra effort involved.

FOEL-GOCH *(Red Bare Hill)*

Return now towards Mynydd Perfedd and, keeping left near the cliffs, look back at the remarkable clean planed slabs which plunge into Cwm Graianog. After passing the windshelter descend to the right easily on grass to re-join the main path from Elidir Fawr and follow it round to beneath the slopes of Foel-goch. The path again seduces you away from an ascent and so must be abandoned and the shaley red screes tackled direct. Three hundred feet of ascent brings you to a ladder stile with a few flat stones for a cairn on the other side, on the end of the spur with a view down Cwm Cywion into the Ogwen valley.

Y GARN *(The Cairn)*

Follow the fence down to Bwlch y Cywion and then up a clear path to Y Garn. The neat top, rough and stony with a semi-circular windshelter, is reached much more quickly than might be expected from its fearsome aspect seen from Mynydd Perfedd. The secret recess of Cwm Clyd looks a delightful place from here. To the north-east the Carneddau are seen end on with the steep and loose slopes of Pen yr Ole Wen dropping straight to Ogwen. To the south-west you can see the little trains chugging up Snowdon.

Follow the edge of the cliffs for about quarter of a mile south-east before turning south to drop towards Llyn y Cŵn, lake of the dogs. The lake is attractively situated with the very steep rocky slopes of Glyder Fawr beyond, whose ascent appears from here to be quite a formidable proposition. The outflow stream, which meanders at first over the moor, drops suddenly and spectacularly over the cliffs of the Devil's Kitchen.

Turn right on an initially clear path before the lake which, after nearly vanishing in a boggy section, re-appears to lead back to the valley. It is a steep and, in places, rocky descent as the path twists and turns its way cleverly down between crags to the left of the Afon Las. Eventually a ladder stile is reached where there is a proliferation of signposts which lead you to the main road. Turn right for the half mile back to Nant Peris.

WALK 2.3 TRYFAN AND THE EASTERN TOPS

SUMMITS:	Tryfan	3002ft (915m)
	Y Foel Goch	2641ft (805m)
	Gallt yr Ogof	2503ft (763m)
DISTANCE:	5¹⁄₂ miles	

ASCENT:	2500 feet
MAPS:	OS Landranger sheet 115
	Explorer OL17 - Snowdon / Yr Wyddfa
STARTING	
POINT:	(115-673604) Gwern Gof Uchaf farm on the A5 just east of
	Llyn Ogwen. Cars may be parked for a small fee.

Of all the summits in Snowdonia which top 3000ft, Tryfan is the lowest. Yet despite only just making it into the first division, Tryfan is one of the finest mountains to be found in the whole of Wales. None of the ways up are less than interesting, as whichever route is chosen, the summit is finally attained only by scrambling. Seen from the A5 approaching Ogwen from Capel Curig, the mountain presents an obvious challenge. The east face buttresses, which give some superb rock climbing, rise to the eponymous three tops in an impressive expanse of rock and at the very apex are the twin monoliths of Adam and Eve silhouetted against the sky. These blocks are so large they can be seen from the road and tradition holds that anyone who jumps from one to the other is made a Freeman of Tryfan. Many thousands have done it, but it isn't as easy as it looks. You have to choose either to jump uphill from the lower to the higher block, or the easier way downhill. The problem with this apparently easier option is that beyond your landing point the mountain falls away immediately in a sheer cliff.

Perhaps the best known of Tryfan's climbing is the Milestone Buttress which abuts the A5 on the north side of the mountain, but the climbs which give a much grander feel of the mountain are those rising from the Heather Terrace. The terrace is clearly in view from the valley and slopes high up across the east face gradually rising from right to left. Among the easier climbs which start from the Terrace, Grooved Arête is one of the finest with its crux pitch, the Knight's Move Slab. The start is easily identified with the letters GA marked on the rocks at the foot of the climb. The one disappointment of Grooved Arête is that it doesn't lead directly to the summit. The climbs on Central Buttress however, such as Pinnacle Rib with Thomson's Chimney to follow, finish right at the top of the mountain.

Tryfan is popular with people of all ages, as all ways up are difficult enough to be interesting without being beyond the ability of most. On one visit we met Ian, a blind lad who was spending three days in attempting all the 3000ft tops, on a sponsored walk to raise money for Operation Raleigh. With infinite patience his companions were describing each step and supporting his moves. His pleasure at being on the top of Adam, was a delight.

ROUTE DESCRIPTION

TRYFAN *(Three Tops)*
Passing to the left of the farmhouse of Gwern Gof Uchaf, a ladder stile leads

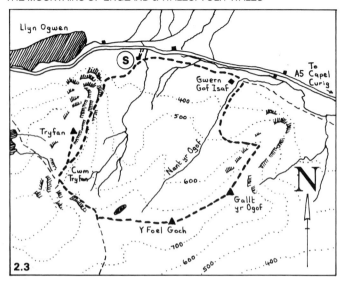

to the hillside and a path going south-west towards Tryfan Bach, Little Tryfan, whose easy angled slabs are frequently used as a training ground for aspiring rock climbers. The path continues, aiming towards the north ridge which falls steeply towards Llyn Ogwen. The ascent of this, although steep, is a popular scramble rather than a rock climb and it is all too easy to miss the start of the Heather Terrace and find oneself embarked on an unintended ascent. The gently rising terrace slants high across the east face and can be clearly seen from the A5 approaching Ogwen from Capel Curig. The start must be carefully watched for, but once on the path it leads with no difficulty or diversions to the col between Tryfan's summit and the Far South Peak where a wall is crossed at a ladder stile. En route the path passes the foot of many of the celebrated east face climbs.

The south ridge from the col, although the easiest route to the top, is nevertheless a scramble over large boulders with one rather exposed move near the edge when the top is just within reach. Strong men have been known to crawl at this point when storm-force winds threaten to hurl them over the edge, but usually there is no problem and you may not even notice it. Nevertheless it is said that Tryfan is the only mountain in Wales that cannot be ascended without the use of hands, although no doubt many people have proved this wrong!

The summit is easily identified. Apart from the fact that it is quite small in extent, it has the magnificent monoliths of Adam and Eve right at the very top.

Y FOEL GOCH *(The Red Bare Hill)*

Having perhaps resolved to do the jump from Adam to Eve another time, the onward route is back, down to the col to the stout wall crossed by a ladder stile. From here a path descends south, going below the Far South Peak to Bwlch Tryfan to join the Miner's Track, which was the route from Bethesda to the Snowdon copper mines. The path descends to contour across the head of Cwm Tryfan, then climbs gradually to break out onto the grassy slopes above by Llyn Caseg-fraith, lake of the dappled mare. One of the classic photographs of Tryfan is with this sheet of water as a foreground. A path on the south side of the lake climbs gently eastwards to pass right over the summit of Y Foel Goch whose highest point is crowned with a cairn on the grassy top to the left of the path. To the east there is a good aerial view of the twin lakes of Llynnau Mymbyr, while to the north-east Llyn Cowlyd can just be seen between the ridge of Creigiau Gleision and Pen Llithrig-y-wrâch.

GALLT YR OGOF *(Cliff of the Cave)*

The continuation to Gallt yr Ogof is a very easy walk over grass and a complete contrast to the rocks of Tryfan whose east face is well seen across the cwm. The summit is a rocky rise crowned with a small cairn and marks the start of the narrowing north-east ridge to which the name properly belongs, which descends gradually towards the Ogwen valley before a final precipitous plunge over cliffs at the end.

The ridge initially provides a good route, but after no more than a third of a mile, it is necessary to turn left down the north-western flank into Cwm Gwern Gof. The tempting path, which continues along the ridge spells disaster or a difficult traverse of rocky heather slopes to escape the trap of the cliffs at its northern end. Rough slopes give way to easier moorland in the valley beside Nant yr Ogof, which is followed down to the farm of Gwern Gof Isaf.

A gate to the right of the farm is on the old Holyhead road along the valley and this leads through a field, which is usually full of tents, and continues to reach Gwern Gof Uchaf in a little under a mile.

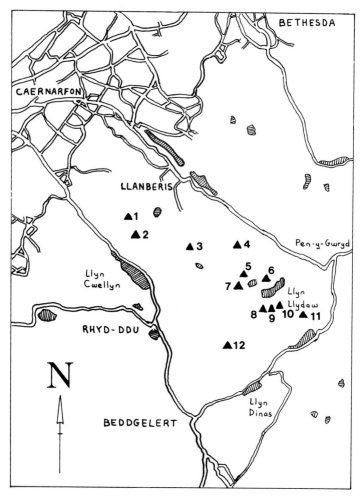

3. SNOWDON

CHAPTER 3: SNOWDON

TOP	NAME	HEIGHT	GRID REF	WALK No.
1	Moel Eilio	726m	115-556577 SH	3.2
2	Foel Gron	629m	115-560569 SH	3.2
3	Moel Cynghorion	674m	115-587564 SH	3.2
4	Llechog	718m	115-606568 SH	3.2
5	Crib y Ddysgl	1065m	115-611552 SH	3.1
6	Crib Goch	923m	115-624552 SH	3.1
7	Snowdon	1085m	115-610544 SH	3.1
8	Y Lliwedd	898m	115-622533 SH	3.1
9	Y Lliwedd East Peak	893m	115-624533 SH	3.1
10	Lliwedd Bach	818m	115-628532 SH	3.1
11	Gallt y Wenallt	619m	115-642533 SH	3.1
12	Yr Aran	747m	115-604515 SH	3.3

Crib Goch

Y Lliwedd from Capel Curig

WALK 3.1 THE SNOWDON HORSESHOE

SUMMITS:	Crib Goch	3028ft (923m)
	Crib y Ddysgl	3494ft (1065m)
	Snowdon	3560ft (1085m)
	Y Lliwedd	2946ft (898m)
	Y Lliwedd East Peak	2930ft (893m)
	Lliwedd Bach	2684ft (818m)
	Gallt y Wenallt	2031ft (619m)

DISTANCE: 8 miles

ASCENT: 3750 feet

MAPS: OS Landranger sheet 115
Explorer OL17 - Snowdon / Yr Wyddfa

STARTING
POINT: (115-647556) Pen-y-pass. Car park (fee). In summer there is
a bus service from Llanberis.

The view of Y Lliwedd and Snowdon seen from Capel Curig on a winter morning
with the snow-capped tops reflected in Llynnau Mymbyr, or at sunset with the
mountains' black silhouette and the orange afterglow shining on the water, is
one of the most perfectly composed mountain scenes in the whole of Wales.
From whichever direction Snowdon is approached, the size and grandeur
of the mountain attracts and dominates the attention. With Snowdon at the
centre, six ridges radiate outwards with subsidiary summits on all but the
western arm and the traverse of the eastern ridges, which form the Snowdon
Horseshoe, is without doubt the finest ridge walk in Wales. The scenery is
magnificent and on the narrow arête of Crib Goch you are on the edge of
all things. It is not an easy walk, as the route is in places very exposed, but
nevertheless it is well within the capability of most walkers providing a fine
dry day is chosen. In winter, when covered with snow and ice, it is only for
those with winter climbing experience.

The whole area enclosed by the horseshoe, reputedly the wettest place
in Europe with over 200 inches of rain some years, was at one time very
industrial. The Miner's Track, a much easier approach to Snowdon than the
ridge of Crib Goch, was constructed to serve the copper mine on the shores
of Glaslyn beneath the east face of Snowdon. The dressed ore from the
mine, which was working in 1810, was initially carried by labourers up the
zigzags over Snowdon and from there by sledge to the nearest road, which
was from Caernarfon to Beddgelert. In about 1830 the Llanberis Pass road
was made and the dressed ore carried over the Pig Track to a store house at
Pen-y-pass. Later still in 1856 the Miner's Track was built, the horses and ore being

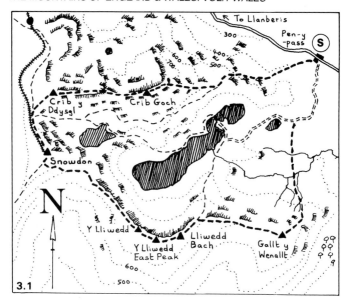

transported on a raft across Llyn Llydaw, Brittany Lake, but after an accident the causeway over Llyn Llydaw was constructed. The Britannia Copper Mine finally closed in 1926.

It is fashionable to denigrate Snowdon as spoilt, whether by the railway, or the café, or the people. This is nonsense. The greasy track winding its way up from Llanberis is unpleasing, but the little train puffing white clouds of steam is somehow quite in-keeping. Among the people thronging the summit there is a feeling of enthusiasm, pride and delight that completely outweighs any minor blemishes.

While a solitary ascent in perfect weather might be thought a daydream, we nevertheless had such an experience while writing this book. Early on a brilliant October morning we climbed the path from Rhyd-Ddu and were the first to see the long crystal splinters of ice that had formed beside the path and arrived at the top unaccompanied. At one time the summit of Snowdon was covered by a huge cairn and its Welsh name, Yr Wyddfa, means the burial place. This is the legendary resting place of Rhita Gawr, a giant killed by King Arthur who is supposed to be asleep, with his knights, in a cave on the face of Y Lliwedd. Around 1820 'a vile wretched hut' was built about 10 yards below the summit, which was the predecessor of the Snowdon Hotel. This is really only a café, in mid-winter it resembles a giant ice lolly, and the only shelter it provides is as a windbreak. It has also the distinction of being the home of the highest house mice in England and Wales.

ROUTE DESCRIPTION

CRIB GOCH *(Red Ridge)*

Take the Pig Track, the broad stony path from the west end of the car park, which leads gently uphill. This track has undergone major reconstruction and gives easy walking with good views down the pass to the twin lakes at Llanberis. After about a mile the path crosses the ridge at Bwlch y Moch, pass of the pigs, probably referring to wild boar hunting, and continues to climb Snowdon contouring round high above the lakes. Turn right at the bwlch and climb steeply up with some scrambling, to the rocky top of Crib Goch. The Snowdon Horseshoe stretches away ahead and you may have to queue here to await your turn for the next section, which is a knife-edge ridge. This can be tackled by the confident by striding masterfully along the very top, and by the timid on all fours. Most people strike a happy medium and shuffle along with their feet a little below the top using the crest as a handrail. The end of the ridge is not in fact the highest point which is about halfway between here and the pinnacles and sometimes marked by a cairn. After this the going is easier.

CRIB Y DDYSGL *(Ridge of the Dish)*

Continue along the ridge now descending to the pinnacles. If possible stay near the crest, it is quicker and easier in the long run, though it is possible to avoid the pinnacles by a long detour to the left. The grassy Bwlch Coch above the lakes of Glaslyn and Llyn Llydaw to the south and Cwm Glas to the north, is at last reached, with a sigh of relief by most people. One hot summer day we saw three rucksacks lifted bodily from the ground by a whirlwind at this spot. The next section is much easier, a pleasant path climbs round to the left of the ridge, but after this it is a question of picking the best line up to the summit with more scrambling involved. Again it is by far the best plan to keep as near to the crest as possible, the inviting little paths that lead off to the left present more difficulties than they avoid. If it is misty the concrete OS trig point looming up on the flat, stony summit is a welcome sight. In good visibility the Crib Goch ridge looks most impressive from here.

SNOWDON or YR WYDDFA *(The Burial Place)*

A short descent on a good path leads to the marker stone at the top of the Pig Track and from here it is an easy walk up beside the railway line to the summit. The highest point is a round OS stone trig point on the top of a rocky knoll, there is also the railway station, the café and lots of other people. The views are tremendous on this the highest mountain of England and Wales, and if you are very fortunate on a fine clear day, it is possible to see Ireland, the Isle of Man and Scafell Pike. There is a jolly sort of holiday atmosphere amongst those who have toiled up on foot and a feeling of superiority towards the mere passengers who arrived by train.

Y LLIWEDD *(The Hue)*

Descend south on the main path for a few yards to an upright marker stone, which in mist is a useful indication of where to turn off, and then zigzag left down the scree to Bwlch y Saethau, pass of the arrows, where King Arthur was slain. Continuing along the ridge, in half a mile at Bwlch Ciliau the Watkin Path goes right, but the horseshoe follows the edge of the cliffs to climb steeply up to Y Lliwedd. There is a good path all the way but the best views are to be had by keeping to the top of the cliffs. The rocky summit is topped by a cairn.

Y LLIWEDD EAST PEAK

A short descent and an ascent of about 70ft leads to the second summit, a

Y Lliwedd from the Pyg Track

rough stony top with a cairn. The cliffs below were very popular with rock climbers at one time, but lately have fallen out of favour, partly perhaps because it is too far to walk, but mainly because of the much higher quality climbing on Clogwyn Du'r Arddu.

LLIWEDD BACH *(Little Lliwedd)*

The top third of Lliwedd is about 300 yards east along the ridge after a descent of around 250ft. The OS somewhat misleadingly have a spot height just before the true col which appears at first sight to disqualify Lliwedd Bach, but this top, which looks quite striking from the Miner's Track, with a re-ascent of 67ft is confirmed as a worthy member.

GALLT Y WENALLT *(Hill of the White Hillside)*

The classic horseshoe route continues descending steeply for a little further until a flattish grassy area is reached where the path to Pen-y-pass turns left to leave the ridge. You will probably have the next section to yourself, as this summit, though geographically part of the Snowdon Horseshoe is not included in the traditional walk. It looks a long way to the last nail in the horseshoe, but the walking is very easy over grass with a faint path to follow. After winding up and down for about three-quarters of a mile, the rocky summit with its little cairn is reached surprisingly quickly. Beneath is the steepest and longest continual slope in Snowdonia stretching down to the Afon Glaslyn.

Walk along the north-east ridge for a few yards and then descend steeply over grass, picking an easy route as there is no path, to a beautiful deserted valley marred only by the pipeline carrying water to the power station in the valley below. Aim to the right of Craig Aderyn, beyond the Afon Glaslyn, then cross the pipeline and climb up to join the Miner's Track to the right of Clogwyn Pen Llechen, which leads back to Pen-y-pass in under a mile.

WALK 3.2 WEST OF SNOWDON

SUMMITS:	Llechog	2356ft (718m)
	Moel Cynghorion	2211ft (674m)
	Foel Gron	2064ft (629m)
	Moel Eilio	2382ft (726m)
DISTANCE:	10 miles	
ASCENT:	3700 feet	
MAPS:	OS Landranger sheet 115	
	Explorer OL17 - Snowdon / Yr Wyddfa	
STARTING POINT:	(115-583597) Llanberis, Snowdon Mountain Railway Station. Several car parks nearby.	

Llechog gazes down in lonely isolation on the Llanberis Pass nearly 2000ft below and although just a few yards from the track of the Snowdon Mountain Railway, it is probably visited by only a very small percentage of the walkers toiling up this route. The three grassy tops which end in Moel Eilio out to the west have more obvious appeal, being clearly separated from the bulk of Snowdon, but they too receive scant attention compared to the better known summits, despite their nearness to two of the popular routes up Snowdon.

The ascent of Snowdon by way of the Llanberis path is easy and straightforward as it follows a clear main stony track all the way. This was the old pony route when Victorian ladies rode to the top. Although it is not the most exciting way up, it is enlivened by the continual interest of the Snowdon Railway which runs close by the path throughout. This is the only rack railway in Britain and rises through a height of 3140ft in a distance of only four miles. It was first opened on Easter Monday in 1896, but a tragic accident, the only fatality ever to occur on the railway, marred the celebrations. Two trains had safely gained the summit and were starting to descend when the engine of the leading train lost control and began to run ahead. The carriages were safely stopped but not before a passenger had jumped from the train, being fatally injured in his fall. The following train then ran into the back of the stationary carriages, fortunately without further injury. The railway was re-opened in April 1897 with additional safety features.

Although Snowdon is approached on this walk, the route turns aside to explore beneath the dark and sombre cliffs of Clogwyn Du'r Arddu. However the ascent of Snowdon may be completed and the described route rejoined by descending from the summit on the Snowdon Ranger path.

From Llechog summit

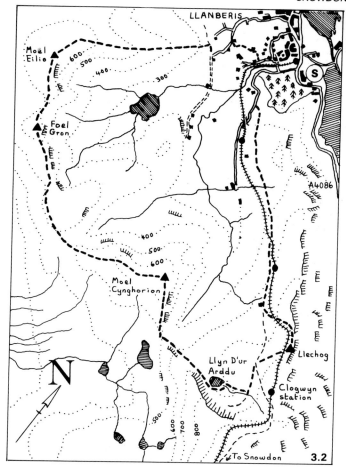

3.2

ROUTE DESCRIPTION

LLECHOG *(Slaty)*

From the Victorian town of Llanberis by the station of the Snowdon Mountain Railway go up Victoria Terrace. After passing the cattle-grid at the end of the houses the steep road gives the first exercise of the day. However it doesn't last long and where the road levels off, turn left through a small gate onto the broad signposted path to Snowdon.

The slopes of Moel Eilio and Moel Cynghorion across the valley to the west look a long way off as you toil up the path. On reaching Halfway House, which once again is serving refreshments and for over 70 years was kept by the same family, the path must be left in order to visit Llechog. At first the railway is followed up the slopes, but then climb beyond it onto the ridge and follow this to reach the highest spot which is Llechog, a neat rocky summit with an eagle's-eye view of the Llanberis Pass 2000ft below. The summit is uncairned and is simply the highest rock on the edge of the drop. Across the Llanberis Pass the summits from Elidir Fawr to Glyder Fawr are well seen and on Crib Goch tiny figures may just be made out in silhouette.

MOEL CYNGHORION *(Bare Hill of the Councillors)*
Descend to cross the railway and rejoin the main path, but then instead of climbing with the crowds towards Clogwyn Station, turn off right on the line of an old tramway leading towards Clogwyn Du'r Arddu. In quarter of a mile descend right following the stream down to Llyn Du'r Arddu. Limestone is sandwiched with volcanic rocks in these cliffs and consequently there is a wider variety of flowers here. On the towering black cliffs, highly regarded by climbers, was the first ever recorded rock climb. It was made by William Bingley, a botanist, searching for plants in 1798.

Clogwyn Du'r Arddu

Passing to the left of the lake scramble over boulders to reach the outflow stream and then, as it begins to drop into Cwm Brwynog, look for a line of cairns which marks the best route through the rocks to Bwlch Cwm Brwynog. The path descends gradually to reach the bwlch, where it joins the Snowdon Ranger path which starts from the Snowdon Ranger Youth Hostel beside Llyn Cwellyn and provides an attractive way up Snowdon from the west side. Snowdon Ranger was opened as an inn by a guide in the early nineteenth century and the path was named after him. It saw service as a monastery and then as an hotel before conversion to its present use as a youth hostel.

Ahead across the valley is Y Garn and you can look down on Llyn Ffynnon-y-gwas. From here it is a climb of just over 500ft to the summit of Moel Cynghorion. The walking now is on grass and quite a contrast to the earlier rock and boulders. Keep fairly close to the edge for the view until the top is reached, a flat grassy plateau whose centre is marked with a small pile of quartz stones. The view, although extensive is rather cut off by the flat surroundings.

FOEL GRON *(Round Bare Hill)*

Follow the ridge west and then south-west down to Bwlch Maesgwm, where the wall is crossed at a ladder stile. Staying on the Access Land you follow the wall up and over the top of Foel Goch.

Foel Gron has two tops, of which the second is quarter of a mile further on and considerably higher. Although the first top has a cairn, the true top, a grassy mound close to the edge, is unmarked. The view to the north-east is dominated by Llyn Dwythwch, Llanberis and the quarries of Elidir Fawr.

MOEL EILIO *(Supporting Bare Hill)*

An easy descent to the bwlch is followed by 400ft of ascent to the last top. It is perfectly straightforward on short grass, but usually seems tougher than expected, coming late in the day. The top, which is the highest of this group, has no cairn, but several substantial windshelters.

With our backs to the windshelter a magnificent prospect unfolded before us. We could see the grass at our feet, a few rocks, beyond that a bit of fence, a ladder stile, the rain coming down and thick mist. Last time we could see even less as it was a total white out when it was quite impossible to distinguish ground and sky. The fence then came in very handy as it was the only thing to focus on. It is a good guide in bad weather, although the views nearer the edge are better, but by following the fence at first north and then when it forks, north-east, the line down the north-east ridge towards Llanberis is indicated.

At the foot of the ridge, a track leads right to the road end. Less than quarter of a mile down the road, just before a farm a small gate on the right leads to a footpath which can be followed back into Llanberis taking in a visit to the Ceunant Mawr waterfall. It is little frequented however and the easier, but longer road route back may be preferred.

WALK 3.3 YR ARAN

SUMMITS:	Yr Aran	2451ft (747m)
DISTANCE:	6 miles	
ASCENT:	2300 feet	
MAPS:	OS Landranger sheet 115	
	Explorer OL17 - Snowdon / Yr Wyddfa	
STARTING POINT:	(115-628507) Nantgwynant on the A498, between Llyn Dinas and Llyn Gwynant. Car park, toilets.	

Yr Aran stands as a lonely sentinel at the end of Snowdon's south ridge. Little visited, the hundreds who climb up the Watkin Path barely give it a second glance. However it is a shapely peak, which because of its isolated position makes an excellent choice for a deteriorating day with the many mines and quarries which litter its flanks offering ample opportunities for a gentle potter and exploration when the mist has dropped to cover the tops. But there are many tunnels, chasms and ruins all unfenced and potentially dangerous so TAKE CARE.

The South Snowdon Slate Works, the huge ruined quarry in the centre of Cwm Llan, opened in 1840 and the Snowdon Slate Quarry on Bwlch Cwm Llan in 1870. Fortunately the area has not been spoilt by the quarries which were relatively small scale, the high cost of transporting the slates from them to Porthmadog proved to be uneconomical and they were both closed soon after 1880. Cwm Llan also has many copper mines. The Sygun Copper Mine

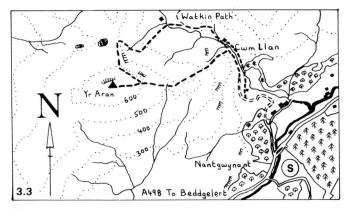

near Beddgelert was opened to visitors in 1986 and gives a fascinating glimpse of the life of a Victorian miner and explains the mining process.

The Watkin Path was built by Sir Edward Watkin, a prosperous railway owner, famous for starting to construct a channel tunnel which had progressed a mile on either side before being thwarted by the government. When he was 70 years of age he built himself a chalet at Nantgwynant, and then, consistent with his ambitious schemes, he extended the miner's road which went to the South Snowdon Slate Quarries up onto the ridge and on to join the Beddgelert path near the summit, so that he had a path from his own house to the top of Snowdon. It was opened by his friend Gladstone in 1892 when he was 83 years old and prime minister for the fourth time.

ROUTE DESCRIPTION

YR ARAN *(The Mountain)*

Take the little lane to the right of Caffi Gwynant, then fork left to follow the edge of the wood. The old mine road winds round crossing an old tramway and climbing up to the left of the waterfalls to reach Cwm Llan in about a mile. On the other side of the Afon Cwm Llan is the ruined processing shop where copper ore was ground down and graded; you can clearly see the position of the water-wheel and feeder stream. Shortly turn left by a trial level to follow a disused incline and then, crossing the old tramway, follow the stream up to another tramway where you turn right to a disused copper mine. Climb steeply up the spoil heaps to ruined mine buildings behind which there is an old level and climb again to a dangerously unfenced chasm, then still higher to gain the ridge. Follow the wall along the ridge to a ladder stile then climb beside an unwelcome electric fence, which has in places encroached upon the path, to the rocky rib of the summit. A cairn crowns the highest point at the far end. The surroundings are dominated by the bulk of Snowdon which looms ahead, while Crib Goch and the Glyders can be seen peeping over the ridge to Y Lliwedd. The lower mountains of the Moel Hebog range, the Moel Siabod range and Mynydd Mawr can also all be seen from here.

The direct descent to the north is awkward, so retrace your steps to the stile and follow the wall left to Bwlch Cwm Llan where the disused slate quarries are full of interest. From the bwlch descend east on the old miner's path which led from the copper mines to Rhyd-Ddu. After a short way turn off left to head for the ruined dressing sheds and workshops of the South Snowdon Slate Works, in whose tips much usable slate remains. Cross the river and follow a grassy path downstream passing below the ruined barracks to join the Watkin Path. You soon pass the 100ft high Gladstone Slab, a practice climbing rock, and next Gladstone Rock upon which Mr Gladstone stood when he declared the path open. Ahead is the remains of the slate quarry manager's house Plascwmllan which was used during the last war as an army training area; the walls are pock-marked by bullets. Just after the house and before crossing the river, go through a gate into the slate fenced enclosure and cross to a small gate. Follow the Afon Cwm Llan past the ruined copper mine buildings and the deep green pools of the falls down to a tiny bridge which crosses high above the river. Slant across the hillside to rejoin your outward route and it is about half a mile back to the start from here.

Mynydd Drws-y-coed, the start of the Nantlle Ridge

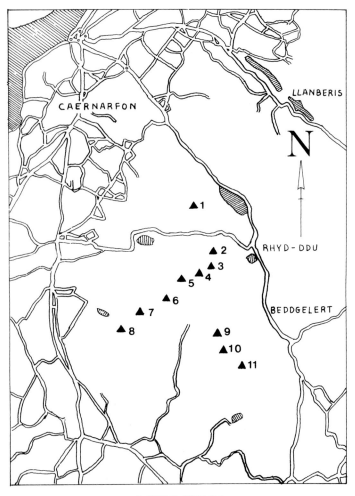

4. MOEL HEBOG

CHAPTER 4: MOEL HEBOG

TOP	NAME	HEIGHT	GRID REF	WALK No.
1	Mynydd Mawr	698m	115-540547 SH	4.3
2	Y Garn	633m	115-551526 SH	4.2
3	Mynydd Drws-y-coed	695m	115-549518 SH	4.2
4	Trum y Ddysgl	709m	115-545516 SH	4.2
5	Mynydd Tal-y-mignedd	653m	115-535514 SH	4.2
6	Craig Cwm Silyn	734m	115-525503 SH	4.2
7	Garnedd-goch	700m	115-511495 SH	4.2
8	Mynydd Graig Goch	610m	115-497485 SH	4.2
9	Moel Lefn	638m	115-553485 SH	4.1
10	Moel yr Ogof	655m	115-556479 SH	4.1
11	Moel Hebog	783m	115-565469 SH	4.1

Jubilee tower on Mynydd Tal-y-mignedd

WALK 4.1 THE MOEL HEBOG RIDGE

SUMMITS:	Moel Hebog	2569ft (783m)
	Moel yr Ogof	2149ft (655m)
	Moel Lefn	2093ft (638m)
DISTANCE:	5¹/₂ miles	
ASCENT:	2800 feet	
MAPS:	OS Landranger sheet 115	
	Explorer OL17 - Snowdon / Yr Wyddfa	
STARTING POINT:	(115-588481) Beddgelert	

Approaching Beddgelert down the attractive Nantgwynant valley from Capel Curig, Moel Hebog is seen rising above the dark green of the forest which covers its lower slopes. To the north it forms a ridge with the lesser heights of Moel yr Ogof and Moel Lefn and although Moel means bald, the hills are far from bare of interest.

Moel yr Ogof takes its name from the cave of Owain Glyndwr who in the fifteenth century led the last uprising of the Welsh against the English, capturing Harlech Castle from Henry IV in 1404. When Wales was re-taken Glyndwr was forced into hiding, taking refuge in this cave high on the mountain after evading his pursuers by swimming the Afon Glaslyn at Nantmor which in those days was tidal and much wider than it is today. Below the cave is an old asbestos mine, reputedly the only one in Great Britain, where the vein of asbestos, a naturally occurring fibrous mineral, can be seen in the roof.

One of Snowdonia's most attractive villages, Beddgelert is famous for Gelert's grave. A heart rending story of a dog mistakenly killed by his master while saving the baby son from a wolf is commemorated by the grave of the faithful hound. Tourists flock to see this from far and wide, but alas it is all a sham as the grave was constructed by David Prichard the landlord of the Goat Hotel in the late eighteenth century in order to boost the tourist trade, and very successful he has been too. Beddgelert also possesses the genuine remains of an Augustinian priory and was at one time very close to the sea which came nearly to the bridge at Aberglaslyn. The retreat of the sea was due to the efforts of William Maddocks who erected an embankment across the mouth of the Afon Glaslyn in 1811, reclaiming land and building the new town of Tremadog and the harbour of Porthmadog.

The network of paths and tracks in the Beddgelert forest is very extensive providing pleasant walking. Few of the paths are shown on the OS map and

Llyn Gwynant

a large scale orienteering map of the area, which is on sale at the campsite, is very useful. There are also orienteering courses in the forest which make an introduction to the sport and an interesting alternative to a day's walking.

The walk starts from the splendid new Beddgelert station of the reopened Welsh Highland Railway which runs from Caernarfon to Porthmadog. The section from Snowdon Ranger to Rhyd-Ddu, which was later known as Snowdon South, was opened in 1881; this linked up with the Beddgelert line but the last passenger train ran in 1916. Re-opened in 1922 by the Welsh Highland Railway, who followed the old route and extended the line

63

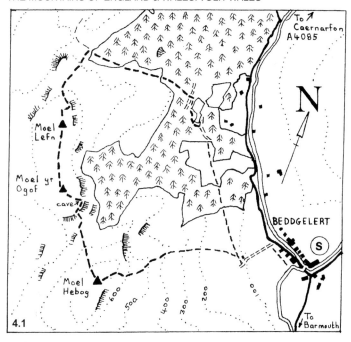

4.1

to Porthmadog, it was not a financial success closing after only 15 years in 1937. However all of the twenty-five mile line should be finished by 2009.

ROUTE DESCRIPTION

MOEL HEBOG *(Bare Hill of the Falcon)*

Take the path to the right of the Royal Goat then keep straight on along the lower path and follow the track past Beddgelert Station and continue below the railway. You walk under the bridge, past the water tank, and follow the path to the left of the stream. Joining a track cross the railway a couple of times then, beyond the farm, turn right through the bridlegate. The footpath forks left then you cross a ladder stile and head up the hill, through the bracken, to another ladder stile.

The path climbs steeply up the hill, first over grass with little rocky knolls, then higher up becoming stony as the ridge narrows. It is well defined and marked with cairns. To the right, across Cwm Bleiddiaid, Moel Hebog throws down an impressive rocky ridge. After about 1000ft of ascent the path turns right and becomes rocky and rather eroded. Keep a lookout for the 'volcanic bombs', an interesting geological formation where lumps of rock thrown up by a volcano millions of years ago lie beside the path. After a further 300ft of ascent the ridges merge and the path turns left. From here you may be able to spot the position of Owain Glyndwr's cave.

The final part of the ridge is very attractive with a steep drop to the left, but then the angle eases and the plateau-like summit comes as a bit of an anticlimax after such a steep ascent. A short walk over grass leads to the highest point which is crossed by a wall with an OS trig point beside it. The views are extensive, with Snowdon the main object of interest across the valley to the north-east. To the south-east are the distinctive shapes of Cnicht and the Moelwyns, while to the south-west lie Tremadog Bay, Caernarfon Bay and the Lleyn Peninsula.

MOEL YR OGOF (Bare Hill of the Cave)
Follow the wall down north-west, initially over grass and then rocks to Bwlch Meillionen, clover pass, a good spot in which to hunt for alpine flowers. From here a direct ascent through a rocky cleft will lead to the next summit, but in order to visit the cave which was the temporary refuge of Owain Glyndwr it is necessary to contour to the right above the cliffs. Climb first up the steep section from the col and then follow the cliff edge rightwards for about 200 yards until a steep gully is reached. An opening at the foot of the cliff on the far side of the gully is the site of an old asbestos mine while the cave itself is at the top of the steep grassy ramp. The route to the cave looks highly precarious and cannot be recommended to walkers. However the old mine is accessible and worth a look.

The summit is reached from here by a short ascent heading west. It is a neat rocky top with a rather untidy cairn. The view to the south is dominated by the bulk of Moel Hebog, while far below is the Pennant valley to the west and the Beddgelert forest to the east.

MOEL LEFN (Smooth Bare Hill)
A faint path leads directly the half mile to the next summit over grass with only 200ft of ascent. To the left the mountain ends abruptly and the land is then flat to the sea. A new fence across the ridge can best be tackled where it abuts the old wall. The summit area is crowned by a huge jumble of rocks. There are two tops, the northernmost being the highest with a small cairn. Straight ahead outlined against the sky on the crest of the Nantlle ridge is the Victoria Jubilee Tower.

To descend, aim to the left of a third rocky tor and head north over grass until you reach the edge of the steep drop where a faint path comes up from the right. Follow this gently downhill north-east and soon it bends to the left heading steeply downhill to the left of a huge slab of rock with a white strip of quartz running through it, and then over loose rock to Bwlch Sais, the Englishman's pass.

From Bwlch Sais continue north-east along the right-hand side of the ridge and then descend steeply over grass. TAKE CARE, the huge chasm of Princess Quarry must be passed on the left to meet a wall. Turn left along the wall and follow it down to enter the trees at a stile at Bwlch Cwm-trwsgl.

A broad path descends gently through the trees to meet a forest road. Turn left and then right at a blue waymark to follow the pretty little narrow path which winds through the forest to emerge again onto the open hillside. Cross the rough open country, with Llyn Llywelyn on your left, for about one quarter of a mile and then re-enter the forest where a path drops steeply through rather gloomy trees. Continue downhill till you meet the bridleway, then turn right, back to Beddgelert.

WALK 4.2 THE NANTLLE RIDGE

SUMMITS:	Y Garn	2077ft (633m)
	Mynydd Drws-y-coed	2280ft (695m)
	Trum y Ddysgl	2326ft (709m)
	Mynydd Tal-y-mignedd	2142ft (653m)
	Craig Cwm Silyn	2408ft (734m)
	Garnedd-goch	2297ft (700m)
	Mynydd Graig Goch	2000ft (610m)
DISTANCE:	13 miles	
ASCENT:	4800 feet	
MAPS:	OS Landranger sheet 115	
	Explorer OL17 - Snowdon / Yr Wyddfa	
STARTING POINT:	(115-572525) The village of Rhyd-Ddu on the A4085 about 4 miles north of Beddgelert. Car park and toilets.	

This long airy ridge is one of the finest high level ridge walks in Wales. Flanked on the south by the Pennant valley and on the north by the Nantlle valley, a succession of six mountains stretches for nearly six miles only once dropping below the 2000ft contour. At the end of the ridge is Mynydd Graig Goch which, after a survey by Leica Geosystems, just scrapes in as a mountain and this is the last outpost before the land dips westwards to the sea.

The main problem confronting walkers of the Nantlle ridge is how best to return to the starting point. A double crossing is one possibility while pre-arranged transport makes an easy day of it. Another solution is to climb Garnedd-goch and

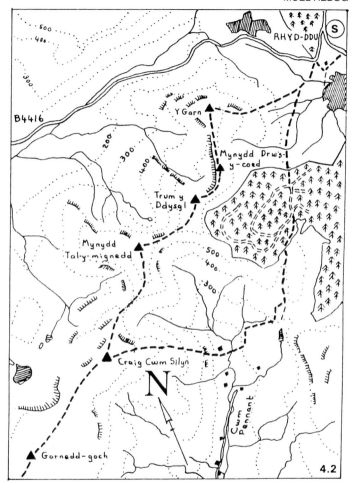

Map labels: S, RHYD-DDU, B4416, Y Garn, Mynydd Drws-y-coed, Trum y Ddysgl, Mynydd Tal-y-mignedd, Craig Cwm Silyn, Garnedd-goch, Cwm Pennant, N, 4.2

Mynydd Graig Goch as a separate walk, starting from Llyn Cwm Dulyn. The route we have chosen however is to descend to the head of the Pennant valley and return through deserted quarries and over a pass into the Beddgelert Forest.

The Prince of Wales Quarry is an eerie place with the remains of the quarrymen's barracks, old winding houses, deep holes and tunnels. It employed

200 men in 1873 but was abandoned in 1882 after a rock fall in which lives were lost. The path at its highest point crosses Bwlch-y-Ddwy-elor, pass of two biers, which is an old corpse road. The two biers referred to an arrangement whereby the coffin, which was to be carried over the pass to the next valley for burial, was met at the parish boundary by men with another bier to carry it down.

ROUTE DESCRIPTION

Y GARN (The Cairn)

Go through the kissing gate on the Beddgelert to Caernarfon road opposite the car park. A slate flagged footpath heads across the fields to a whitewashed house, Tan y Llyn, with Y Garn, the first peak of the Nantlle ridge beyond. Turn left in front of the house and cross the Afon Gwyrfai at a footbridge to join a track. Follow this until it joins the road from Rhyd-Ddu to Nantlle at the bend and then immediately take the bridleway that heads south-west towards Y Garn. A stile is reached and the footpaths on the hillside beyond have been marked with white arrows painted on the rocks. Ignoring the arrows to left and right climb steeply uphill following white arrows until you leave the farmer's land. A clear path climbs straight to the summit over grass with excellent views of the steep rocky face which the mountain turns towards Mynydd Mawr. This ascent of nearly 1500ft is probably the hardest climb of the walk. Nearing the summit the substantial stone wall is crossed at a ladder stile.

On the summit there are two huge ancient cairns which have been hollowed out forming wind shelters, but the highest point is the small untidy cairn at the northern end of the ridge on a little promontory. There is a magnificent view of the ridge stretching away ahead. A wall runs along the edge of the steep drop to the Nantlle valley, and you can look straight down onto the valley below.

MYNYDD DRWS-Y-COED (Door to the Wood Mountain)

Follow the ridge, which is initially grassy, to the towering bulk of Mynydd Drws-y-coed ahead. Keeping near to the steep drop on your right climb up over rough rocks and boulders picking the easiest line to the top. The ascent is one of the best bits of the whole walk with enjoyable scrambling and excellent situations and it comes as a surprise to find that the top of the rocks is not in fact the summit. This is a little further on, an area of smooth grass just beyond the ladder stile without even a cairn. Quite an anticlimax in fact.

The views from here are very extensive. Ahead lies the rest of the Nantlle ridge with Caernarfon Bay on the right and Moel Hebog to the left. Far below in the Nantlle valley is Llyn Nantlle Uchaf and to the north across the valley is Mynydd Mawr. The Snowdon range dominates the eastern view while to the south-east is Cnicht and the Moelwyns with the Arenigs in the far distance. The stretch of water which can be glimpsed to the south-east just right of the Moelwyns is Trawsfynydd Lake and beyond that are the Arans, while to the south the Rhinogs complete the panorama.

TRUM Y DDYSGL *(Ridge of the Dish)*

From Mynydd Drws-y-coed a truly alpine path with a tremendous drop to the right leads down to the col and then climbs steeply up to Trum y Ddysgl. For the thirsty a detour along a path at the col leads to a spring. The easy climb up is less than 200ft and you quickly reach your third summit which is at the northern end of the flat, broad, grassy sweep; it has no cairn.

MYNYDD TAL-Y-MIGNEDD *(Mountain at the End of the Bog)*

Walk across the smooth grass of Trum y Ddysgl top to the southern end, then head south-west down over grass to the col, a delightful spot with steep drops on either hand. An easy walk up, again over grass, joins and follows a wall to the summit with its tall stone tower, built by quarry workers to commemorate Queen Victoria's Diamond Jubilee. Some restoration work had taken place on our last visit and the top had been raised by a couple of feet.

CRAIG CWM SILYN *(Silyn Valley Crag)*

Follow the fence south down the wide grassy ridge until it narrows and then slither down a slippery path to the broad grassy col of Bwlch Dros-bern. From here the huge bulk of Craig Cwm Silyn towers overhead; it looks a long way up. Follow the fence up to a steep rocky buttress where the path detours round to the right to make an easy ascent slanting back to the ridge. A good path then picks its way through the rocks and, staying close to the edge, climbs steeply straight to the summit area, finally crossing a boulder field to arrive at the highest point, a hollowed-out ancient cairn. The top is a broad, stony ridge and about 200 yards beyond the cairn is the remains of a square tower-like structure. The high mountains of Snowdonia look a long way away from here.

GARNEDD-GOCH *(Red Cairn)*

Head west passing the ruined tower and, shortly beyond, the remains of two more to a rocky tor where there is an eagle's-eye view of Cwm Silyn with its twin lakes far below. Then skirting the steep drop to your right, head south-west straight for the wall which leads directly to the top. The way is at first grassy, but as it become more stony keep right on a cairned path to avoid the worst of the rough ground. The summit is a huge pile of jumbled rocks crowned by a truncated OS trig point at the junction of two walls.

MYNYDD GRAIG GOCH *(Red Rocky Mountain)*

The valley ahead is dominated by a tall TV mast and you now head for the final peak, a mile further on. Follow the south side of the wall, cross the semi-ruined wall and descend to the grassy col of Bwlch Cwmdulyn, then climb the slope to the summit. The highest point is a rocky pinnacle on the east side of the wall.

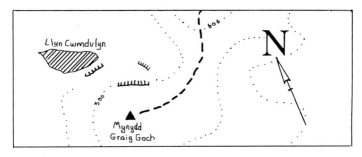

Return to Craig Cwm Silyn, past the summit and then when the path veers left leave it to follow the ridge descending over boulders to locate the top of the south-east ridge. After a short initial stony section easy grassy slopes, with a precipitous drop on the left, lead down to join a stone wall. Cross this at the first ladder stile and continue beside it until the ground steepens. The easiest line is now away from the wall beside a gully over steep, grassy slopes to reach the ruined cottage in the valley below. Cross the head of Cwm Pennant to a bridge and then climb steeply beside the fence for 300ft to an old dismantled railway track. This track, which ran from here for five miles to join the Porthmadog Railway, closed in 1894. Turn left on the track for a short way and then right, after the embankment, to climb to the ruined Prince of Wales Quarry over grassy slopes. Follow the path up to Bwlch-y-Ddwy-elor through the quarry, which though full of interest has some dangerous unfenced chasms. The track then descends through the Beddgelert Forest to join a forest road. Crossing the forest on these roads, turning first left then straight across the next junction, leave it at a small gate and follow the footpath back to Rhyd-Ddu.

WALK 4.3 MYNYDD MAWR

SUMMITS: Mynydd Mawr   2290ft (698m)

DISTANCE: 6¹/₂ miles

ASCENT: 1850 feet

MAPS: OS Landranger sheet 115
              Explorer OL17 - Snowdon / Yr Wyddfa

STARTING
POINT: (115-572525) The village of Rhyd-Ddu, on the A4085 about 4
             miles north of Beddgelert. Car park and toilets.

Above the hamlet of Rhyd-Ddu stands the lonely summit of Mynydd Mawr. Isolated from the mountains to the south by Bwlchgylfin, the pass on the Rhyd-Ddu to Nantlle road, the mountain rises steeply on all sides defended on three of them by cliffs. When seen from Llyn Cwellyn, Mynydd Mawr is supposed to resemble an elephant, but its most interesting aspect is from the south, where the shattered granite cliffs of Craig y Bera, seen in the light of the setting sun shining up the valley, look very fine indeed. The summit is a surprisingly good viewpoint for many of the mountains of northern Snowdonia with even the Carneddau visible away to the east.

The ascent described follows the eastern ridge above the cliffs with magnificent views down the crumbling gullies. Although the quickest way back to Rhyd-Ddu is to return the same way, a more interesting alternative is to descend to the shores of Llyn Cwellyn past the overhanging cliffs of Castell Cidwm, wolf castle. This castell was at one time thought to be an ancient British fort, but is now known to be a purely natural formation. The precipitous face provides climbers with some hard routes.

Llyn Cwellyn is a very deep lake in which can be found many trout and also the char which is a rare deep water fish. On the opposite shore is the

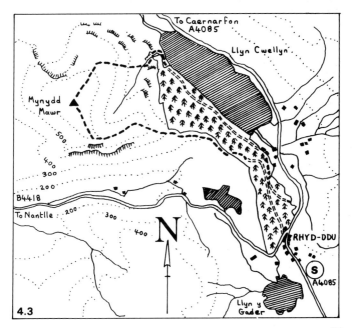

Craig y Bera from the Nantlle valley

Snowdon Ranger, now a youth hostel but at one time a place from which a guide could be hired for the ascent of Snowdon.

ROUTE DESCRIPTION

MYNYDD MAWR *(Big Mountain)*

From the car park walk through the little village of Rhyd-Ddu. After passing the Cwellyn Arms on Stryd Edward (the A4085), turn left up the B4418, then right after Cefn Cwellyn along a forest road. After about three-quarters of a mile the road becomes a footpath which turns left to climb up through the trees, under a power line. Reaching the top of the forest at a ladder stile Llyn y Dywarchen Reservoir can be seen below on the left. Turn right and follow the edge of the forest and then climb the steep grassy east ridge of Mynydd Mawr to Foel Rûdd which gives commanding views.

The ascent is now more gentle and follows the top edge of Craig y Bera. Continue to climb above the shattered cliffs, with spectacular views down the gullies to the once industrial Drws-y-coed and across to Y Garn where the entrances of old mines can be seen on the steep hillside. The path then turns away north-west to climb gently to the grassy summit which is capped with a large stony area that surely must be natural, though it is also the site of an ancient cairn. There are several wind shelters to suit all sizes of parties, and the remains of the Bronze Age cairn. The westwards horizon takes in Anglesey and Cardigan Bay, but the chief attraction is the mountain panorama. The Nantlle ridge dominates the view southwards with Moel Hebog just appearing behind. To the south-east are the Moelwyns while eastwards lies Snowdon with the Glyders beyond and the Carneddau in the distance.

Unless you are returning by the route of ascent, head north-east towards Moel Eilio in the distance, over easy grass, to the col before Craig Cwmbychan. Heather-covered slopes slant down eastwards to the forest and Llyn Cwellyn far below. A small stream is a guide to the best route down, with a slithery intermittent path on its north side. Sadly aircraft remains still lie in this gully, relics of the last war, and are to be found all the way down. Before the stream joins the Afon Gôch, cross over and traverse the heathery slopes to join the far grassy bank thus avoiding an awkward descent by a waterfall. The lower part of this secluded valley is a lovely area with Llyn Cwellyn below and Snowdon opposite, very remote and hidden with only the climbing cliffs of Castell Cidwm to attract other people.

Make your way down to the shores of the lake and then, after passing the disused quarry, return along the forest road beside the lake for about a mile to a barn and a stile by a gate. Now leave the track and follow the edge of the forest to a small gate into the trees by a fire notice. Enter the wood and fork left immediately along a path which leads south gently uphill for about 200 yards until it peters out by a broken wall. Turn right and climb up to join the forest road followed at the start of the walk. From here it is about half a mile back to Rhyd-Ddu.

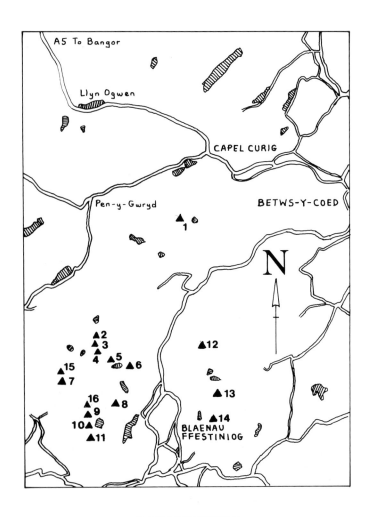

5. THE MOELWYNS

CHAPTER 5: THE MOELWYNS

TOP	NAME	HEIGHT	GRID REF	WALK No.
1	Moel Siabod	872m	115-705546 SH	5.1
2	Ysgafell Wen Far North Top	650m	115-664488 SH	5.2
3	Ysgafell Wen North Top	669m	115-664486 SH	5.2
4	Ysgafell Wen	672m	115-667481 SH	5.2
5	Moel Druman	676m	115-672476 SH	5.2
6	Allt-fawr	698m	115-682475 SH	5.2
7	Cnicht	689m	115-645466 SH	5.3
8	Moel-yr-hydd	648m	115-672454 SH	5.3
9	Moelwyn Mawr	770m	124-658449 SH	5.3
10	Craigysgafn	689m	124-660443 SH	5.3
11	Moelwyn Bach	710m	124-660437 SH	5.3
12	Moel Penamnen	620m	115-717483 SH	5.4
13	Manod Mawr North Top	658m	115-728458 SH	5.4
14	Manod Mawr	661m	124-724447 SH	5.4
15	Cnicht North Top	686m	115-648469 SH	5.3
16	Moelwyn Mawr North Ridge Top	646m	124-661453 SH	5.3

Barracks in Rhosydd quarry

Moel Siabod

WALK 5.1 MOEL SIABOD

SUMMITS:	Moel Siabod	2861ft (872m)
DISTANCE:	6 miles	
ASCENT:	2400 feet	
MAPS:	OS Landranger sheet 115	
	Explorer OL17 - Snowdon / Yr Wyddfa	
	Explorer OL18 - Harlech, Porthmadog & Bala / Y Bala	
STARTING POINT:	(115-735571) Layby on the A5 to the east of Pont Cyfyng, about 1 mile east of Capel Curig.	

Moel Siabod is an isolated mountain dominating Betws-y-Coed and the surrounding countryside of woods and lakes. Rising steeply from small forest hills it presents its best side to the south-east, a long ridge flanked by cliffs, and looking every inch of its 2861ft. The approach from this direction lives up to the promise with a spectacular rocky cirque, formed by glacial action, enclosing an attractive lake followed by a steep scramble up the east ridge which leads directly to the summit. The northern aspect of Moel Siabod is less rugged with mainly grassy slopes sweeping down to the twin lakes of Llynnau Mymbyr where, across the A5 and overlooking the lakes, stands the farmhouse Dyffryn Mymbyr, the home of Thomas Firbank when he wrote *I Bought a Mountain*. In the bogs on the southern side, the rare grass of Parnassus can be found. This looks rather like a white wood anemone, but has five petals and heart-shaped leaves. Moel Siabod is its most southerly habitat in Wales.

The small village of Capel Curig is very popular with walkers as there are two outdoor pursuits shops as well as a post office cum café, wool shop, youth hostel, hotel, and of course Plas y Brenin, the National Centre for Mountain Activities. This was formerly the Capel Curig Inn built in 1800 and renamed the Royal Hotel because of its many royal visitors. The inn was taken over by the army during the Second World War and became an outdoor pursuits centre in 1955.

We spent many pleasant camping holidays at Betws-y-Coed when our children were small. The weather is kinder here than in the high mountains and the forest walks more suitable for short legs. Most visits included an ascent of Moel Siabod, indeed our youngest went to the top in a rucksack aged only six weeks.

ROUTE DESCRIPTION

MOEL SIABOD

Cross Pont Cyfyng, a narrow bridge, and take the second footpath to the right,

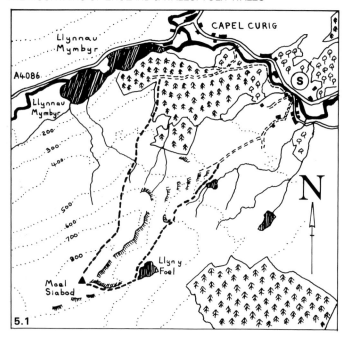

CAPEL CURIG

Llynnau Mymbyr

A4086

Llynnau Mymbyr

200
300
400
500
600
700
800

Llyn y Foel

Moel Siabod

N

5.1

beginning as a private tarmac road. The road winds uphill past some cottages, then continues as an unsurfaced track towards Moel Siabod, past an attractive little lake, to Rhos Quarry. Like most of the other slate quarries in Snowdonia this is now derelict but at one time 45 men worked here; it closed in the 1950's. Pass to the left of a deep green quarry pool and skirting round the fenced edge, a good signposted path climbs to a col and then goes to the right of Llyn y Foel crossing a rather boggy area. From here the east ridge, Daiar Ddu, climbs directly to Moel Siabod summit. This is a delightful ascent, an easy scramble up a narrow rocky arête, with a good path all the way. The flat, stony summit has a rocky knoll on the highest point with an OS trig point. The views are extensive, with the Snowdon Horseshoe, the Glyders and the Carneddau to the west and north being the main focus of attention, a great contrast to the wide panorama of the low ground to the east.

A large windshelter, once used as a pen for tourists' ponies, gives the direction of descent. The north-east ridge can be followed along its stony crest above the cwm, but the way is much easier to the left on short grass. Just

Llyn y Foel from the East Ridge of Moel Siabod

before the angle steepens, by a grassy rake and a bit of stone wall, a faint path sets off steeply downhill northwards, becoming more distinct and marked with cairns lower down. This is the Plas y Brenin path, which crosses a ladder stile at a fence corner and descends to the edge of the forest. The path continues through the trees to join a forest road after about half a mile. Turn right and in a further half mile a forest road comes in from the left. In 50 yards fork right to take the track which leads beside the river. This becomes a footpath leading to the footbridge at Cobdens Hotel. Don't cross but continue to follow the river through fields to a barn. From here waymarks guide the way to stepping-stones below a cottage and back to Pont Cyfyng.

WALK 5.2 NORTH WEST OF BLAENAU FFESTINIOG

SUMMITS:	Allt-fawr	2290ft (698m)
	Moel Druman	2218ft (676m)
	Ysgafell Wen	2205ft (672m)
	Ysgafell Wen North Top	2195ft (669m)
	Ysgafell Wen Far North Top	2133ft (650m)

DISTANCE: 7¹/₂ miles

ASCENT: 1900 feet

MAPS: OS Landranger sheet 115
Explorer OL17 - Snowdon / Yr Wyddfa
Explorer OL18 - Harlech, Porthmadog & Bala / Y Bala

STARTING
POINT: (115-701488) The A470 at the top of the Crimea Pass, 2 miles
north of Blaenau Ffestiniog. Car parking in a layby.

Between the slate mining town of Blaenau Ffestiniog to the south and Moel
Siabod above Capel Curig to the north lies a beautiful area of small lakes
and knolls. The summits are not in themselves the chief attractions, but they
are set amid delectable surroundings. Confusing in mist, the area is best
visited on a clear day when detours of exploration can be made and the
views appreciated. It is on the edge of an industrial region much quarried in
the past, indeed some of the lakes were used as reservoirs for the Rhosydd
Slate Quarry at Bwlch Cwmorthin.

The A470 crosses the Crimea Pass between Dolwyddelan and Blaenau
Ffestiniog, rising to a height of over 1200ft. Named after an inn that once stood
there, its proper Welsh name is Bwlch y Gorddinan. The two big quarries
that stand on either side of the road where it descends to Blaenau Ffestiniog
are now open to tourists. Llechwedd on the east, which has been working
since 1849, has little trains to take the visitor through the caverns. Gloddfa
Ganol Slate Mine on the other side of the road was originally known as the
Oakley Slate Quarry. It closed in 1971 to be re-opened in 1974 for small-
scale quarrying and as a tourist attraction where quarrymen's cottages, a
slate museum and a working slate mill can be visited.

Dolwyddelan, a large village by the River Lledr was once too a quarrying
centre. Today there is little to see of its early importance but it was crossed
by Sarn Helen, a Roman road and it also has a Welsh castle dating from
1170 which stands dramatically on a rocky outcrop. Llewelyn the Great
was probably born here as the castle was built by his father. In 1283 it was
captured by Edward I and refortified.

A railway line runs down the Lledr valley beside the river and the main

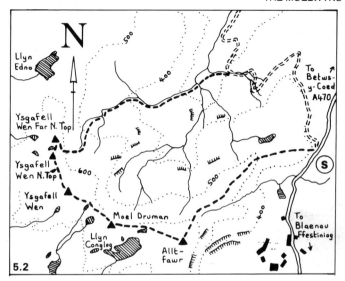

road and shortly before it plunges into a tunnel under the mountains it passes Roman Bridge Station where there is a bridge, which though very old is certainly not Roman.

ROUTE DESCRIPTION

ALLT-FAWR *(Big Hill)*

Take the track that heads north from the summit of the Crimea Pass and immediately leave it to climb west up the steep grassy slopes to the left of an old trial level, aiming for the stile silhouetted on the skyline. From here there is a bird's-eye view of Blaenau Ffestiniog and Allt-fawr can be seen ahead. Follow the fence on its north side to cross a stile above Llyn Dyrnogydd, then take a faint path, which passing to the left of a rocky outcrop, continues for about a mile along the ridge to the col. Below lies Llyn Iwerddon and the path continues up the north-east ridge of Allt-fawr, fading out before the highest point, a rocky rib. In clear weather there is a good view of the Moelwyns to the south-west while the path westward to Moel Druman follows the ridge which can be seen curving away towards Moel Siabod in the distance.

MOEL DRUMAN *(Bare Hill Ridge)*

Continue along the ridge for 50 yards to the lowest point, then pick up an

Bridge over the Afon Lledr

improving path that heads west to pass to the right of the little lake north of Llyn Conglog along a rocky rib. Llyn Conglog was extended in 1870 to form a reservoir to provide additional water power for the quarry below at Bwlch Cwmorthin. This area is very deceptive in mist as the tiniest of lakes looks endless, but once the path to the north of the lakes has been located the rest of the navigation is simple. Follow the path for about a quarter of a mile and then strike up to the right to the flat, rocky and grassy summit of Moel Druman which has no cairn. This is a beautiful viewpoint for the Moelwyns and Cnicht, Snowdon and the Dolwyddelan valley.

YSGAFELL WEN *(White Ledge)*
Continue west to rejoin the path which descends to Llyn Coch. Here a line of old fence posts leads past Llyn Terfyn, past scree slopes, then bends left to a high point at a col, where you scramble up rocky slopes to the summit on your right. This neat rocky top has a small pile of stones on the obvious highest point.

YSGAFELL WEN NORTH TOP
Return to the fence and follow it for nearly half a mile, past another little lake to the first high point, where the posts are set into the rock and climb left to

the summit. The rocky top, marked by a small cairn, unusually has patches of thyme and some golden rod growing on the sparse grass. There are good views of Yr Aran, Y Lliwedd and Snowdon.

YSGAFELL WEN FAR NORTH TOP

Only 200 yards north is the third summit of Ysgafell Wen. The OS map gives little hint of its presence with only a single ring contour, but a short, sharp ascent of over 50ft brings you to a fine rocky pinnacle, topped by a cairn, which is well deserving of inclusion.

Return to the col and descend over easy slopes north-east into the valley of the infant Afon Lledr. Follow the river down for a mile and a half, past old mine workings and little ravines, to a wide, flat, open area. On the far side a path leads from a ruined farm to join an old track for a last couple of miles of easy walking, passing the spoil heaps of the railway tunnel and the airshaft on a beautifully engineered track, in places blasted from the rock, back to the summit of the Crimea Pass.

WALK 5.3 CNICHT AND THE MOELWYNS

SUMMITS:	Cnicht	2260ft (689m)
	Cnicht North Top	2251ft (686m)
	Moel -yr-hydd	2126ft (648m)
	Moelwyn Mawr North Ridge Top	2119ft (646m)
	Moelwyn Mawr	2526ft (770m)
	Craigysgafn	2260ft (689m)
	Moelwyn Bach	2329ft (710m)

DISTANCE: 9½ miles

ASCENT: 3760 feet

MAPS: OS Landranger sheet 115 & 124
Explorer OL17 - Snowdon / Yr Wyddfa
Explorer OL18 - Harlech, Porthmadog & Bala / Y Bala

STARTING
POINT: (124-631447) Croesor village, 4 miles north of Penrhyn-deudraeth. Car park.

Cnicht, the Welsh Matterhorn, is a favourite mountain for many visitors to the little village of Croesor and although on attaining the summit it is found to be merely the end of a ridge rather than the shapely peak seen from below, the ascent is so enjoyable that the deception can be forgiven. Croesor, which is remotely situated at the end of a minor road north of Penrhyndeudraeth,

**Adit, Rhosydd
quarry**

consists of only a few houses and a chapel, but it still has a school, a reminder of its busy quarry days. For the super energetic the walk can be extended by adding the tops north-west of Blaenau Ffestiniog (Walk 5.2) before descending past the ruined Rhosydd Quarry to the Moelwyn range.

Rhosydd Slate Quarry is a fascinating place where one can spend hours exploring. Commenced in 1840 the quarry, which in its heyday employed about 200 men, started originally at a height of 1850ft. The huge chasm known as the West Twll, west hole, was excavated first and as the depth increased the associated buildings moved lower down the mountainside. Thus a succession of mills, barracks and adits each constructed at a different stage of the quarry's development can be seen. Later underground chambers were quarried and a smaller open quarry, the East Twll, which collapsed in the Great Fall of 1900. The most recent buildings are to be found on the bwlch where a 2221ft long adit, the Lefel Fawr, leads through the heart of the hillside

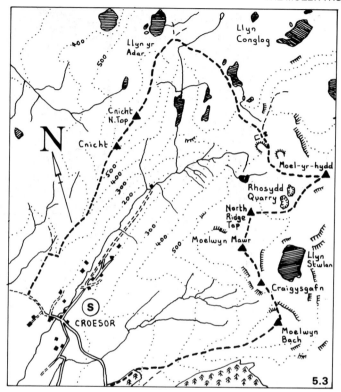

5.3

to connect with the bottom of the West Twll. This adit took about eight years to complete. Walkers are warned that it is dangerous in the underground workings, there are unfenced precipices and frequent roof falls as the whole area is unstable.

The principal source of power for the quarry was water, which was cheap and plentiful. Many of the nearby lakes show clear evidence of being harnessed to supply the quarry and as the excavations deepened the higher adits were supplanted by lower ones. The disused adits were dammed at both ends to form yet more reservoirs. The dams have been removed from the highest adit, but the one below, to which it was connected by a 90ft shaft, is still holding water. Further buildings are to be found in Cwmorthin below to the east where the manager's house, which was built in 1860, was lived in until

1930. There is a row of cottages and a chapel built in 1867 used as a school. The quarry closed in 1930, though men worked producing roofing slates from the wall consequently much ruined.

To the west lies Cwm Croesor and the Croesor underground with the Rhosydd. Hydroelectric powe Cwm-y-foel which drove the machinery, lit the tunn for haulage in the main tunnel of the quarry. This same time as Rhosydd though it was later used tramway from Rhosydd Quarry to the end of t opened in 1864. The incline is most impressive a: 671ft. Worked purely by gravity the drum and cabi.

Modern times have also left their mark on these heart of the Moelwyns lies Llyn Stwlan which is part of th pumped storage scheme. The power station is sitec Reservoir 1000ft below.

ROUTE DESCRIPTION

CNICHT *(Knight)*

Take the lane which leaves Croesor past the school and chapel to climb uphill to a gate. Continue north along a track to the brow of the hill where you fork right, the track continuing towards the shapely peak of Cnicht which appears ahead. At a ruin, after half a mile, turn right over a ladder stile then follow the concession path along the ridge all the way to the summit. It is a delightful path with a short scrambly section but nowhere difficult. It joins the rocky summit ridge at the highest point which is sometimes marked by a small cairn. There is an extensive panorama from the next objective the Moelwyns to Moel Hebog and the Nantlle ridge, the Snowdon massive, the Glyders and Moel Siabod over to the lesser tops north-west of Blaenau Ffestiniog.

CNICHT NORTH TOP

Heading north it is easy to miss Cnicht's northern summit, as we did until Dewi Jones told us about it, for the path sneaks off to the side, but it is the work of only a moment to pay one's respects. This new summit is crowned by an untidy cairn.

MOEL YR-HYDD *(Bare Hill of the Stag)*

A gentle stroll down the north-east ridge of Cnicht, for about a mile, leads to a cairn at the col with Llyn yr Adar, lake of the birds, to the left. Turn right at the cairn which marks the path south and from here it is about another mile to Bwlch y Rhosydd and the deserted quarries. This whole area is very confusing in mist and the path is indistinct in places. Llyn Cwm-corsiog, which has been extended to form a reservoir for the Rhosydd Quarry is passed and just above the bwlch is another reservoir, now dry. The bwlch and part of the opposite hillside are covered with the fascinating remains of the Rhosydd Slate Quarry. To the left are the men's barracks and to the right the ruined mill of which little remains as the walls were pushed over and split to form roofing slates. Passing between the two buildings and to the right of the deep Lefel Fawr adit, climb the disused incline to the drumhouse, walk a short way along the track then climb a second incline to another drumhouse. Straight ahead you can see the remains of an earlier barracks and the entrance to an earlier adit which has been sealed to form a reservoir. Continue up to the left through the dressing waste of a former mill which you pass to the right and climb left up the final incline to join a disused railway track.

You are now at the top of the quarry with the unfenced chasms of East and West Twll ahead. Turn left by a small building to take a faint path which leads directly to the summit of Moel yr-hydd. (The main track continues past a former reservoir to a still earlier mill and an earlier adit and finally to the chasm of the West Twll, by which stand the very first quarry buildings.) There is no cairn on this little-visited grassy and rocky top high above Blaenau Ffestiniog. The Ffestiniog Railway snakes below beside the lake and there is a good view of the new tunnel which had to be constructed when the Tanygrisiau Reservoir flooded the original line.

MOELWYN MAWR NORTH RIDGE TOP
Descend the west ridge of Moel yr-hydd and pass to the left of the West Twll. Then by continuing west you can pick up the northern ridge of Moelwyn Mawr and visit this recently discovered top which, as its discoverer Myrddyn Phillips points out, has some fine rocky teeth.

MOELWYN MAWR *(Big White Bare Hill)*
It is then only another 400ft to the flat summit of Moelwyn Mawr where an OS trig point is perched on the brink of the cliffs above Cwm Croesor with its quarry and old tramway.

CRAIGYSGAFN *(Rock Stack)*
A good path leads down the south ridge of Moelwyn Mawr to cross this minor top. The second rocky tor, which has a cairn, is the highest. Below lies Llyn Stwlan Reservoir.

MOELWYN BACH *(Small White Bare Hill)*
The path continues to Bwlch Stwlan and climbs to the left of the crags across the screes and then over grass to the summit, an easy ascent of 400ft. The flat, rocky top has a cairn on the highest point from which the Rhinogs can be seen beyond Llyn Trawsfynydd.

The west ridge of this final summit leads straight back to the minor road to Croesor. After a mile, head for the north edge of a wood where an attractive path leads through the trees to the lane. Turn right for an easy half mile walk back to the village.

WALK 5.4 EAST OF BLAENAU FFESTINIOG

SUMMITS:	Moel Penamnen	2034ft (620m)
	Manod Mawr North Top	2159ft (658m)
	Manod Mawr	2169ft (661m)
DISTANCE:	7¹/₂ miles	
ASCENT:	2150 feet	
MAPS:	OS Landranger sheets 115 & 124	
	Explorer OL18 - Harlech, Porthmadog & Bala / Y Bala	
STARTING POINT:	(115-702459) Blaenau Ffestiniog.	
	There is a car park in the town centre, toilets.	

The mountains to the east of Blaenau Ffestiniog are dominated by the quarries. The hills have been scoured and gouged, tunnelled, quarried and blasted and just when we thought all this was in the past it has started again. The once attractive lake between the tops of Manod Mawr has been spoilt by bulldozers driving a new track and is now a muddy pond. It is very sad, yet even in the desolation there is a fascination in the industrial archaeology, with abandoned trucks stacked with finished slates and inclines, with steel cables and drums still in position. While on the slate tips there is still hope with the pale pink flowers of the stonecrop colonising the bare ground.

Blaenau Ffestiniog is the centre of a huge slate mining area. Once a busy industrial town, most of the quarries are now disused and though the slate waste has mellowed with time it can be a dark and dismal place, especially on a misty, wet day. The original town was Ffestiniog, a couple of miles down the valley, but with the advent of the slate quarries, Blaenau Ffestiniog was born. It has the unfortunate claim to fame of being the wettest town in Britain with an average rainfall of about 100 inches, indeed of nearly 150 inches in one particularly wet year. We have seen it in all weathers. On our first walk up through the quarries we missed a great deal of interest as the ground was covered with a thick blanket of snow. This was on Easter Sunday after a visit to the bilingual church. Prayers alternated between Welsh and English but hymns were sung in one's own native tongue, both languages at once. Mysteriously the Welsh version always seemed to have an extra verse. However it doesn't rain all the time and we have stayed at Ffestiniog when it was so hot that meals were eaten out of doors and the whole place, decorated with window boxes of flowers, had a continental air.

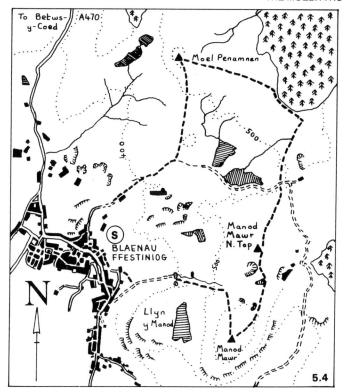

5.4

In the centre of the Blaenau Ffestiniog car park, in splendid isolation, stands an unusual building. This is at present alas used as public conveniences, but a second glance reveals it is in fact the old ticket office of the narrow-gauge railway. The railway was opened in 1836, then the line was improved so that by 1840 the trains could run all the way from here to Porthmadog by gravity. The empty trucks were pulled back up again by horses which travelled down to the coast at the rear of the train in special 'Dandy' carriages. Later steam locomotives were used and it became the first narrow-gauge steam railway in the world.

The walk encircles the quarries to the east of the town, first passing Maen Offeren Quarry which opened in 1861. This was worked underground and was still producing roofing slates in 1972. It is a fascinating place with much

Slate trucks in Maen Offeren quarry

of the old machinery still remaining. Slate from Llechwedd Quarry is now brought here to be worked and also quarrying has recently been resumed at the bwlch between the north and south tops of Manod Mawr. The interior of this mountain has huge hollowed-out caverns which during the last war were used to store art treasures from London at a constant temperature and humidity. After an expensive court case, the owner has now recommenced quarrying so the vaults and Manod Mawr North Top are in danger of vanishing forever. Fortunately the summit is just within the National Park boundary which should offer some protection.

The walk descends by Graig-ddu Quarry, which was the highest quarry in North Wales. A branch line was constructed from the Ffestiniog Railway to the quarry which opened in 1840 and closed in 1946, and was worked in the open. Unlike many of the more remote quarries in North Wales, the men were able to return home each evening. This they did down a series of four inclined planes on small linked trolleys known as ceir gwyllt' or wild cars.

ROUTE DESCRIPTION

MOEL PENAMNEN

From the back of the car park a new tarmac road climbs north shortly to become an unsurfaced track, leading steeply uphill through slate spoil, with high retaining walls on either side. You emerge into the fascinating world of tips, ramps and inclines of the disused Maen Offeren Quarry though the trucks shown in the drawing have now gone. The right of way, somewhat overgrown, passes through the rhododendrons to the left of the ruined manager's house, then zigzags back to the left of the incline, which still has the rails in place, and climbs to the winding house with its cable and drum. Continue to climb north-east to a ruined winding house and cross over a stile by a gate onto the open moor. The summit of Moel Penamnen lies a mile to the north and after following a ruined wall for a short way, head straight across the pathless moor making for the highest point to the right of the steep slope, finally climbing to join the ridge which is followed to the top. The flat, grassy summit with the odd rocky bit has a small cairn and you can look across to Manod Mawr the next top.

MANOD MAWR NORTH TOP

Walk east along the ridge for three-quarters of a mile to the minor hump of Foel-fras and then follow the fence down south-east past a little lake to the forest edge. Turn south at the next fence which leads all the way to the north top of Manod Mawr, just over a mile away. To the right are the reservoirs of Llyn Newydd and Llyn Bowydd, built to provide the quarries with water power and to the left is Cwt-y-bugail Slate Quarry. Crossing a track at the bwlch climb up to Manod Mawr which is quite steep and rocky in places. The fence passes some strange square slate structures roofed with a large flat slate. The fence bends abruptly left on the summit, and the highest point is a few yards to the west. A large cairn perches on the flat, rocky top which is abundantly provided with seats in the form of comfortable rocky ledges tailored to suit all shapes and sizes of walkers in need of a sit down. There is also a notice warning of blasting.

MANOD MAWR *(Large Snowdrift)*

Descend south east keeping to the left of the lakes to avoid the surprisingly close quarry workings and the freshly bulldozed roads which scar the bwlch. The south top lies an easy three-quarters of a mile away with a gentle ascent over grass to the summit of grass and rough boulders topped by a windshelter, but the trig point has gone. It is however an excellent viewpoint dominated to the west by the Moelwyns above the Tanygrisiau Reservoir; to the south is Llyn Trawsfynydd and the Rhinogs.

Descend north to the ruined Graig-ddu Quarry and follow the old incline down passing between two lakes at its foot. Turn right through the ruined buildings and descend a second disused incline, through a waste of slate which is covered in summer with the pale pink flowers of the stonecrop. Just before a gate there is a small stile across the fence to the right and a waymarked path leads towards Blaenau Ffestiniog downhill to a ladder stile. Cross a little lane and follow a track past a few cottages and along a path back high above the houses to the town centre.

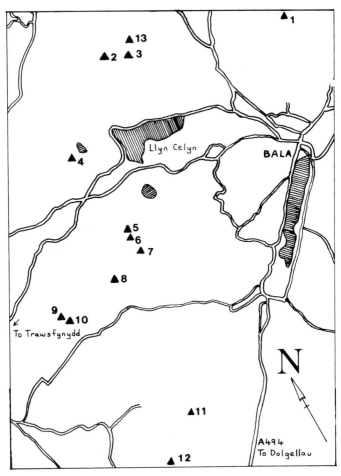

6. THE ARENIGS

CHAPTER 6: THE ARENIGS

TOP	NAME	HEIGHT	GRID REF	WALK No.
1	Foel Goch	611m	125-954423 SH	6.4
2	Carnedd Llechwedd-llyfn	643m	124-858445 SH	6.2
3	Carnedd y Filiast	669m	124-871446 SH	6.2
4	Arenig Fach	689m	124-820416 SH	6.2
5	Arenig Fawr	854m	124-827370 SH	6.1
6	Arenig Fawr South Top	836m	124-827366 SH	6.1
7	Arenig Fawr South Ridge Top	712m	124-827360 SH	6.1
8	Moel Llyfnant	751m	124-808351 SH	6.1
9	Gallt y Daren	619m	124-778345 SH	6.1
10	Foel Boeth	616m	124-779342 SH	6.1
11	Dduallt	662m	124-810274 SH	6.3
12·	Rhobell Fawr	734m	124-787257 SH	6.3
13	Waun Garnedd-y-filiast	650m	124-874452 SH	6.2

Sheep on Dduallt

Arenig Fawr and Llyn Arenig Fawr

WALK 6.1 ARENIG FAWR

SUMMITS:	Arenig Fawr	2802ft (854m)
	Arenig Fawr South Top	2743ft (836m)
	Arenig Fawr South Ridge Top	2336ft (712m)
	Moel Llyfnant	2464ft (751m)
	Foel Boeth	2021ft (616m)
	Gallt y Daren	2031ft (619m)
DISTANCE:	11½ miles	
ASCENT:	3300 feet	
MAPS:	OS Landranger sheet 124	
	Explorer OL18 - Harlech, Porthmadog & Bala / Y Bala	
STARTING POINT:	(124-823392) One mile west of Arenig village on the minor road off the A4212 to the south of Llyn Celyn. Ample parking beside the road.	

To the west of Bala and flanking Llyn Celyn and the fast main road to Trawsfynydd, Arenig Fach stands guard to the north while Arenig Fawr, the principal top, is to the south. The area is predominantly grassy moorland, quiet and unfrequented, but easier walking than the heather moor of the Berwyns to the east.

Arenig Fawr, the big Arenig, is by far the grandest mountain of this range. George Borrow in *Wild Wales* 1854 said "Of all the hills which I saw in Wales none made a greater impression on me." A strange sentiment with which, despite the undoubted worth of Arenig Fawr, very few would agree. Towering 2800ft above sea level it dominates the surrounding countryside. Appearing to receive more than its fair share of mist and rain, averaging 77 inches a year over Llyn Celyn, holly lake, it took three visits before we were able to see the mountains. Third time lucky, we at last had good visibility and were able to sort out the position of ridges and tops which before were very confusing. The mountain seemed even bigger and more rugged when we could see it all.

Perhaps the most scenic way up is via the east ridge above Llyn Arenig Fawr, but this adds a good two miles of road and track to the walk. The more direct ascent given is much quicker and has the added advantage of being completely safe in mist, of which there is a great deal, as a fence leads directly from the valley bottom to the summit.

The south ridge of Arenig Fawr descends gradually to an area of small lakes, where a minor top achieves the 2000ft criteria. Across the valley to the west is Moel Llyfnant whose rocky top comes as a nice surprise after the grassy flog up, while further west and with the forest fast approaching on several sides is Foel Boeth.

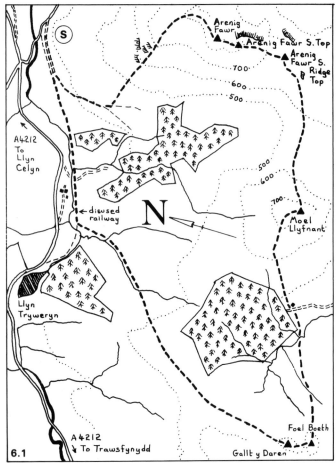

6.1

The walk returns along the disused single track railway which ran from Blaenau Ffestiniog to Bala. This wound its way high up across the moors to the hamlet of Arenig at the northern foot of Arenig Fawr, which had its own railway station. The ascent of Arenig Fawr was a favourite with day trippers. Now the hills of Snowdonia have the greater appeal and few of those hurtling along the A4212, to those popular mountain summits and the crowded seaside, stop here.

Arenig Fawr from the disused railway

ROUTE DESCRIPTION

ARENIG FAWR *(Large High Ground)*

Take the No Through Road beside the dismantled railway line going south-west. After half a mile the track swings away from the railway uphill to the south passing a disused quarry. In another half mile a wall and electric fence meet the track at a gate. Navigation is easy as this fence is followed on its left-hand side all the way up the north-west ridge to the summit. It is initially a steep climb over grass, with extensive views westwards towards the Moelwyns and Rhinogs. An area of shattered rocks on the left is passed and the top of the ridge is soon gained. It is an easy walk of less than a mile from here beside the fence to the summit where there is the OS trig point and a big windshelter constructed from an ancient cairn. The windshelter contains a memorial plaque to the eight-man crew of a Flying Fortress who were killed when it crashed on the Arenig on the 4th August 1943. The views from the top are very extensive to Arenig Fach, Bala Lake and the Berwyns, the Arans and Rhinogs, the Moelwyns and the distant hills of Snowdonia.

ARENIG FAWR SOUTH TOP

The short descent south over grass and re-ascent of around 80ft to the cairned subsidiary summit is straightforward with the fence as a guide in mist.

ARENIG FAWR SOUTH RIDGE TOP

Below to the south the ridge flattens out in an area of small lakes and knolls.

It is about half a mile to the highest of these which, with a rise of 60ft, is another two-thousander. A rough descent beside the fence over boulders to a grassy col with a small tarn, then a short climb to the left gains the cairned top of this rather humble summit.

MOEL LLYFNANT *(Smooth Brook Bare Mountain)*

Return to the fence to avoid the marshy ground, continue south and after passing a large tarn at the lowest point, head west down to the boggy col. A faint path follows steeply up the line of an old wall. As you near the ridge, aim left to the summit. The highest point is the far side of the fence, a rocky knoll topped with a cairn. After a rather tedious ascent the short grass of the summit with its rocky outcrops comes as a pleasant surprise. A stroll south to a little promontory gives a bird's-eye view of the Afon Lliw valley. A fence post just below the summit is neatly signed with the initials MJ, made from bent nails, and a small horseshoe.

FOEL BOETH *(Burnt Bare Mountain)*

Although only a mile north of the minor road from Trawsfynydd to Bala Lake, this area feels very quiet and remote. Descend from Moel Llyfnant following the fence north then north-west to a fence junction. From here head west towards the corner of the infant forest, crossing a track by a ruin where the Outdoor Leisure map shows a non-existent extension of the forest. A stile, left of the forest corner, is most welcome. Aim south of Craig y Ffolt for a ravine which leads up towards the high moor and then west across to the top of Foel Boeth. The highest point, a grassy top with a cairn, is on the north side of the fence, while on the opposite side a truncated telegraph pole which once looked out over the forest against a backdrop of the Rhinogs, now lies on the ground.

GALLT Y DAREN *(Hill of the Knoll)*

The adjacent top, which is slightly higher than Foel Boeth, is about 300 yards north along the fence. Both tops qualify as separate summits with a descent of 55ft followed by a re-ascent of 65ft. The remains of a line of telegraph poles stretch over the moor, one standing forlornly on the col and on the summit are the remnants of an iron mast. There is a little rocky cliff surmounted by a few stones of a cairn at the highest point. Trawsfynydd Lake can be seen from here.

Follow the fence north to Moel y Slates. Just before Bwlch y Bi there is a rocky cliff with a strong foxy-smelling cave. Above this a small cairn marks a faded plaque bearing the inscription "In memory of BONZO the brave fox terrier who perished in this cave after eight days unsuccessful rescue attempt, which took place from April 23 to May 1 1973'. There is a list of those who attempted to dig poor Bonzo out.

From Moel y Slates summit there is a good view of the eight-arched viaduct of the disused railway. Follow the fence north for a short way then descend right to the Nant y Gist-faen which is crossed at a ravine, a spot where another stream joins. Follow the stream down to the permissive path along the old railway line which leads back to the No Through Road.

WALK 6.2 ARENIG FACH

SUMMITS:	Waun Garnedd-y-filiast	2133ft (650m)
	Carnedd y Filiast	2195ft (669m)
	Carnedd Llechwedd-llyfn	2110ft (643m)
	Arenig Fach	2260ft (689m)
DISTANCE:	11½ miles	
ASCENT:	2550 feet	
MAPS:	OS Landranger sheet 125 or 124	
	Explorer OL18 - Harlech, Porthmadog & Bala / Y Bala	
STARTING POINT:	(124-857411) The north side of Llyn Celyn on the A4212. The most westerly layby is the handiest for the start of the walk.	

Arenig Fach is a mountain scarcely noticed by the motorist speeding along the new and improved A4212 to the coast. Dominated by the larger summit of Arenig Fawr on the other side of Llyn Celyn, it resembles a pudding. But Arenig Fach is undeserving of its dull reputation and the approach from the north-east reveals the mountain's better side. Here there are cliffs which fall steeply to the hidden waters of Llyn Arenig Fach and a ridge which leads interestingly to the summit. The adjoining mountain of Carnedd y Filiast is not as grand as its namesake in the Glyders, but the two linked together make a pleasant walk, with a scramble above the lake leading to the summit of Arenig Fach. Between the two summits, and surveyed by the minor top of Carnedd Llechwedd-llyfn, lies the Migneint, which means boggy hollows, a vast area of bog, cotton grass and heather. The poor soil is acid and peaty, with moss and moorgrass, sphagnum, rushes and reeds, a quiet place with a beauty all of its own.

Llyn Celyn is an unnatural stretch of water. The Memorial Chapel built in 1971 commemorates the village of Capel Celyn, which was drowned by Liverpool Corporation's reservoir, completed in 1965. The chapel is a memorial to those buried in the two submerged cemeteries, one of which was an early Quaker burial place. On the main road by the dam, there is a plaque in memory of the Quakers, many of whom emigrated to Pennsylvania. The village comprised a chapel, school, post office and 11 farmhouses and cottages, which were demolished to make way for the 830-acre lake. The main industry of the village was hand-knitting. The hand-spun hosiery and gloves were sold at Bala market and later a woollen mill was set up.

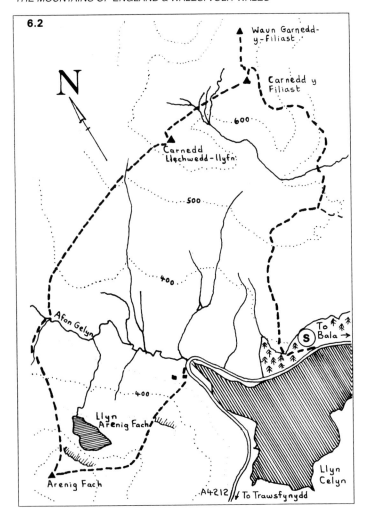

There was much opposition to the construction of the reservoir which destroyed this Welsh-speaking community. Somehow, even on a sunny day there is an air of sadness about the place.

The reservoir was built to conserve the water which flows into the River Dee via the River Tryweryn. This saved water is released when necessary and flows along the natural channel of the Dee all the way to Chester, where it is removed from the river and then travels by aqueduct to Liverpool's reservoir. Because of the facility of controlled water release, Afon Tryweryn has developed into a world class canoeing river with the National White Water Centre situated on the river below the dam.

ROUTE DESCRIPTION

WAUN GARNEDD-Y-FILIAST *(Cairn of the Greyhound Moor)*
From the layby on the A4212, the very busy main road above the shores of Llyn Celyn, walk east for about 300 yards on the fortunately wide grass verge. Arenig Fawr, to the south beyond Llyn Celyn, looks very grand. Just after the bend, take the broad grassy track which slants back up through the forest. This climbs gently through dense woodland to a gateway onto the open mountain. Pass under the pylons, following the track which becomes stony and more obvious as it climbs up through the heather. The view expands as you ascend with Llyn Celyn and Arenig Fawr behind, and the last objective of the day, Arenig Fach, looking a long way away to the west.

After about a mile the track bends round to the right under Foel-boeth and gradually descends for about half a mile to a junction. Fork left and descend more steeply until the track fords the Nant y Coed. This is a pleasant spot with good views into the valley of the Afon Hesgyn and the ridge beyond. From here it is about a mile to the summit. The track climbs up, gradually steepening to meet the ridge where the angle eases. After an indistinct section the track continues to meet a fence where you go right to this minor grassy summit which is topped with a small cairn. In July 1999 Myrddyn, Dewi, two friends and a surveying level spent three hours measuring this top. They concluded it rose by 15.1m, but only 49ft 7½ inches! After much discussion it has been decided that as 50ft has been approximated to 15m (OS maps only give metric contours), and other tops which rise by 15m are included, then Waun Garnedd-y-filiast must join the ranks of the elect

CARNEDD Y FILIAST *(Cairn of the Greyhound)*
Follow the fence back to the col and up to the next summit.

The grassy top is crowned by a large cairn with an adjoining wall shelter, an OS trig point and a boundary stone surrounded by a cairn. These are modern constructions, the stones having been taken from the ancient cairn to which they once belonged. To the south-west are seen the twin peaks of Arenig Fach and Arenig Fawr.

CARNEDD LLECHWEDD-LLYFN *(Cairn of the Smooth Hillside)*
Follow the fence west for nearly a mile over rough tussocky grass to an old shepherds' cairn. Carnedd Llechwedd-llyfn lies about 200 yards south of

here. This is a choose-your-own summit. A few stones poke through the thin grass, but there is no cairn to mark the highest spot. Wherever you stand, somewhere else usually looks higher. However it you tramp about a bit you are bound to have passed over it.

ARENIG FACH *(Small High Ground)*

Return to the fence and follow it west for another couple of miles. The walking is easy with a feeling of great solitude. The occasional boundary stone will be seen in the fence, while to the right lies the vast wilderness of the Migneint, a huge area of bog and heather, some 25 square miles, reputedly the largest of this type in Wales.

Arenig Fach lies ahead with Arenig Fawr partly hidden behind it, while to the left brood the dark waters of Llyn Celyn. The col is rather boggy, but the worst can be avoided by trending left away from the fence to cross the Afon Gelyn at its confluence with the Trinant. An old abandoned wooden farm cart makes a good foreground for photos of the wild landscape.

Follow the Trinant, a lovely little stream, up to its source, keeping to the left branch, and passing close by a massive boulder with a curious cave at its foot. Climb to join the ridge of Arenig Fach above the steep drop to Llyn Arenig Fach which suddenly comes into view. A faint path comes and goes until you reach a cairn at the highest point.

From the top of the cliffs head west to cross an old fence to the summit which is marked by a stone OS trig point, with the remains of an ancient cairn forming a shelter. From here you can look across to its big brother, the more famous Arenig Fawr, and in clear conditions to Snowdon.

To descend, aim east to rejoin the ruined fence and follow this down, at first over rough heather, until above the lake. Then turning north-east over grass and stony outcrops, the main road is joined after one and a half miles at the bend. From here it is a mile back to the layby, passing on the right the memorial chapel to the drowned valley.

WALK 6.3 DDUALLT AND RHOBELL FAWR

SUMMITS:	Dduallt	2172ft (662m)
	Rhobell Fawr	2408ft (734m)
	NOTE: when the river is in spate it is best to remain on the south bank of the Afon Mawddach to avoid recrossing at the ford.	
DISTANCE:	9 miles	
ASCENT:	2250 feet	
MAPS:	OS Landranger Sheet 124	
	Explorer OL23 - Cadair Idris & Llyn Tegid	

STARTING
POINT: (124-787293) 7 miles south-east of Trawsfynydd, in Cwm yr
Allt-lwyd at the end of a minor road where a few cars may
be parked.

The countryside between the Aran ridge and the Coed-y-Brenin Forest is a
very peaceful and little frequented area of rough grass and moor with rocky
summits. Dduallt, when seen from the north, is a very striking mountain with
steep cliffs on the east from the foot of which rises the Afon Dyfrdwy, the River
Dee. Rhobell Fawr is a large craggy lump, and the two are separated by a
chunk of Forestry Commission woodland best described by the orienteering
term FIGHT. This word is applied to woodland through which it is impossible
to run or walk. In these circumstances orienteers sometimes resort to

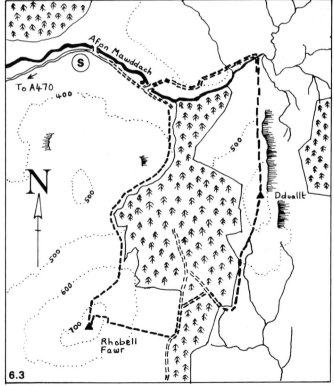

6.3

crawling, which is what we tried with the Rhobell Fawr forest on our first visit. This method cannot be recommended, for not only did we get scratched, but when retreat seemed the only option, there was some doubt as to whether we could retrace our steps. The trees seemed magically to have grown round us, as if we were in some horrid Grimms fairy tale. As fox-hunting was taking place quite close, with much tally hoing, or rather the Welsh equivalent, this all added to the illusion that we were about to perish.

We were not much more fortunate on our second visit. After three days of continuous heavy rain the area was awash and the ford proved too deep to cross. We were thus faced with a lengthy circumnavigation of the headwaters of the Afon Mawddach. This area is boggy at the best of times and we would have been best equipped with goggles and flippers, rather than boots and ice axes. Nevertheless, having gained the mountainside, we had a thoroughly enjoyable day with the hills entirely to ourselves.

Many of the rights of way shown on the map have fallen into disuse or have been planted over with trees. The approach can be made from Dolhendre off the main Bala Dolgellau road, but unless the weather has been dry for a long time the nearly vanished paths are very boggy. The south also gives access to the area but the chosen approach from the north gives the most satisfactory route for a round walk.

ROUTE DESCRIPTION

DDUALLT *(The Black Hillside)*
From the road end walk down the track marked 'Farm and FC vehicles only'. Cross over the Afon Mawddach at a bridge to pass in front of the deserted Allt-lwyd Farm. From here an old right of way leads up to join a bulldozed track which climbs to cross the headwaters of the Afon Mawddach at a ford. The track continues for a short way up onto the end of the north ridge of Dduallt where a fence acts as a guide all the way to the summit. Although the way ahead looks quite rocky and difficult, it is possible to stay on easy, but rough grassy slopes all the time and the top is quickly reached. The little rocky cairn is built on a summit of tussocky grass, bilberry, and scattered rocks, with good views of the Aran ridge, the Arenigs and Rhobell Fawr.

RHOBELL FAWR *(Big Saddle)*
Resist the temptation to head straight for the next summit as the way is barred by dense and impenetrable forest. Instead descend the south ridge, which has little rocky steps and ledges, and it is an easy walk down on grass to the edge of the forest. This is followed to a corner where the forest bends sharp right. Continue along the edge to the next corner where there is a gap in the defences. Follow the narrow ride, which heads north-west through the trees, and then turn left onto a wide grassy ride which leads you through to join the forest road below the slopes of Rhobell Fawr.

Dduallt from the headwaters of Afon Mawddach

Walk left down the track for a short way and then turn right to follow a wall which climbs steeply and almost directly for the summit. As the angle eases, a wall is crossed and then the continuation wall beyond is followed until a second wall is crossed. Turn left to the summit. The highest point is a grassy mound marked by a stone OS trig point.

To descend, follow the wall from the summit north and then cross it to head down the north ridge to the forest. Keep by the edge of the trees, passing close by Foel Gron. A bridleway is joined and this leads down beside the beautiful Nant yr Helig, stream of the willow, which flows over little falls and through deep gorges by the edge of the forest. On reaching the farm track turn left and head back along this to the starting point.

WALK 6.4 FOEL GOCH

SUMMITS:	Foel Goch	2005ft (611m)
DISTANCE:	5¹/₂ miles	
ASCENT:	1100 feet	
MAPS:	OS Landranger sheet 125	
	Explorer OL18 - Harlech, Porthmadog & Bala / Y Bala	
STARTING POINT:	(125-962397) A corner in the minor road which runs north-west from Cefn-ddwysarn on the A494, 3 miles north-east of Bala. Restricted parking by the roadside.	

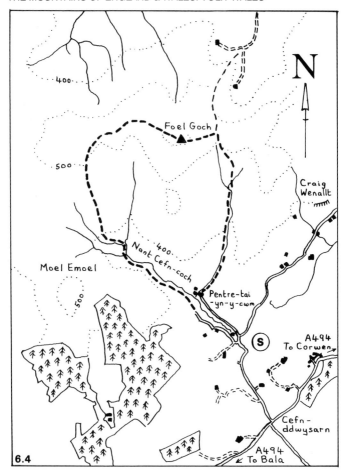

While Arenig Fawr and Arenig Fach are close neighbours, divided only by the gloomy waters of Llyn Celyn, Foel Goch is the distant relation separated from the rest of the group and standing in lonely isolation away to the east. Because of this isolation the mountain is usually climbed, if at all, in combination with other lesser tops, an incidental to the main purpose of the walk, or perhaps as an excursion for an odd few hours. So while longer walks can be devised in this pleasant and little frequented area, taking in say Moel Emoel to the south-west, the walk described makes a pleasant half day tour of this solitary top.

ROUTE DESCRIPTION

FOEL GOCH *(Red Bare Hill)*

A narrow lane to Pentre-tai-yn-y-cwm runs north-west from the corner of the minor road where beside the road is a cracked slate, bearing the single word 'Pentre'. When the lane ends at the farm, turn right in front of a ruined cottage up a grassy lane. The track soon emerges onto the hillside which is covered in yellow gorse and shortly crosses a wooden bridge to gain the left bank of the stream. Foel Goch now comes into view across the moor where patches of heather mark the drier areas. Little remains of the path but follow the stream until it is crossed again to a gate, at which point the old trackway re-appears and starts to climb more resolutely until the top of the pass is reached at a marker stone inscribed Llanfor on one side and Llangwm on the other.

Turn left, crossing the fence at a stile, up the broad slopes of Foel Goch. A pathless but easy climb of around 300ft over grass leads to the top in under half a mile. The neat grassy summit has in close proximity an OS trig point, a boundary stone and a cairn. As Foel Goch is isolated from other hills, as well as quiet walking over deserted hills, there are good views. Northwards is the extensive Clocaenog Forest and north-west the distant hills of northern Snowdonia. Westwards is Llyn Celyn flanked by Arenig Fach and Arenig Fawr, while far beyond is the distinctive outline of the Moelwyns. To the south the Arans appear beyond Bala Lake, Llyn Tegid, and to the south-east are the rolling heather hills of the Berwyn range.

A series of boundary stones follows the ridge westwards towards Garnedd Fawr, and these provide guiding points for the descent, but the walking is easy enough anywhere on the high ground. As the slopes of Garnedd Fawr are reached at the second col, contour round the reedy head of the cwm by a sheepfold and follow the broad ridge of Foel Fâch leading due south to the confluence of three streams which feed the Nant Cefn-coch. Cross to a gate and a grassy track on the south side of the Nant Cefn-coch. The track is followed to the first farm where the surface becomes metalled and then continues downhill back to the minor road a few yards from the start.

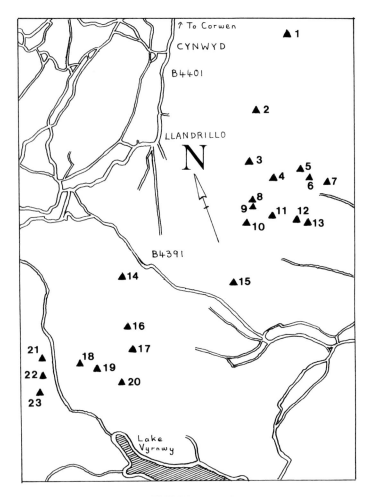

7. THE BERWYNS

CHAPTER 7: THE BERWYNS

TOP	NAME	HEIGHT	GRID REF	WALK No.
1	Moel Fferna	630m	125-117398 SJ	7.1
2	Pen Bwlch Llandrillo Top	621m	125-090369 SJ	7.1
3	Cadair Bronwen	785m	125-077346 SJ	7.1
4	Foel Wen	691m	125-099334 SJ	7.2
5	Tomle	742m	125-085335 SJ	7.2
6	Foel Wen South Top	687m	125-103330 SJ	7.2
7	Mynydd Tarw	681m	125-113324 SJ	7.2
8	Cadair Berwyn	827m	125-072327 SJ	7.2
9	Cadair Berwyn New Top	830m	125-072324 SJ	7.2
10	Moel Sych	827m	125-066318 SJ	7.2
11	Moel yr Ewig	695m	125-081318 SJ	7.2
12	Godor North Top	675m	125-089311 SJ	7.2
13	Godor	679m	125-095307 SJ	7.2
14	Foel Cwm Sian Llŵyd	648m	125-996314 SH	7.4
15	Post Gwyn	665m	125-049294 SJ	7.3
16	Y Groes Fagl	659m	125-988290 SH	7.5
17	Cyrniau Nod	667m	125-989279 SH	7.5
18	Pen y Boncyn Trefeilw	646m	125-963283 SH	7.5
19	Stac Rhos	630m	125-969279 SH	7.5
20	Cefn Gwyntog	615m	125-976266 SH	7.5
21	Foel Goch	613m	125-943291 SH	7.5
22	Trum y Gwragedd	612m	125-941284 SH	7.5
23	Foel y Geifr	626m	125-937275 SH	7.5

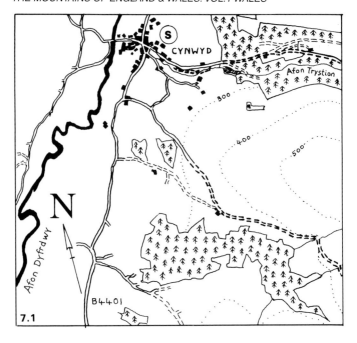

WALK 7.1 THE NORTHERN BERWYNS

SUMMITS:	Moel Fferna	2067ft (630m)
	Pen Bwlch Llandrillo Top	2037ft (621m)

DISTANCE: 12 miles

ASCENT: 2200 feet

MAPS: OS Landranger sheet 125, Explorer 255

STARTING
POINT: (125-056411) The village of Cynwyd on the B4401, 2 miles south-west of Corwen. There is a small car park and toilets in the centre of the village.

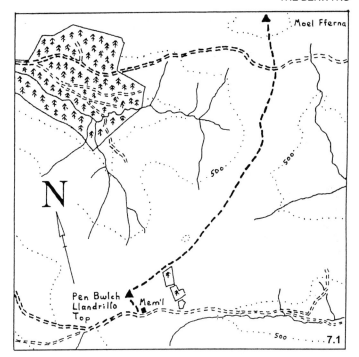

The Berwyns, an area of high moorland to the east of Bala, extends some 15 miles from Moel Fferna in the north to the undulating hills around the Penllyn forest in the south-west. Much of the range is thickly covered in heather and although this is a delight when in flower it will be cursed by anyone having to force a route through it. Fortunately a path has developed alongside the fence which follows the main watershed of the northern Berwyns and this walk presents little difficulty. Fences form the few boundaries to be found on the Berwyns, the shaley rock being unsuitable for building walls.

The western flanks of the Berwyn range slope gently down to the River Dee. Although in places the hills are densely afforested, several of the forest roads can be used to gain access to the ridge. These roads sometimes run close to or upon the ancient trackways that crossed from east to west and are consequently rights of way. One of these, Ffordd Saeson, the Englishmen's road, leads from Cynwyd towards England. It is thought to be the route taken by the retreating army of Henry II in 1169, when defeated by the Welsh weather, he fled from Owain Gwynedd.

Another old trackway runs from Hendwr by the Dee to the attractive little village of Llanarmon Dyffryn Ceiriog. At its highest point, Bwlch Llandrillo, 1900ft, stands a memorial to 'A Wayfarer 1877-1956, a lover of Wales' a well-known cyclist who often visited here. There is a visitor's book in a cache and the col has been christened 'The Wayfarer's Pass' by the Wayfarer Cycle Touring Club, Isle of Wight. The club left a birthday card in the visitor's book to their namesake on their fifth birthday and second visit to the memorial stone, on 23rd May 1988. Other visitors included a Duke of Edinburgh Award group who left a note 'Time of arrival 2.40. Leaving time 2.42. Clare looks very tired, she looks like she's going to faint with the weight of the rucksac'. Poor Clare! Owain Glyndwr is reputed to have used this pass as a route between two of his estates in the thirteenth century.

Moel Fferna, over two miles north of its nearest neighbour, would not usually merit great attention, a single ascent being sufficient to add it to the list. However, rough heather and the difficulty of linking it satisfactorily to other summits, when combined with farmers' reluctant to admit the existence of rights of way, has resulted in numerous ascents and this summit becoming an old friend of ours. In all conditions we have plodded up Moel Fferna from every direction (the ascent by the north-west ridge is not recommended unless you have a particular fondness for knee-deep heather). Approaching the top in March we stopped in surprise. The trig point had vanished. In its place was a neat wall shelter built from the stones of the ancient cairn, but

The trig point on Moel Fferna

almost hidden away among the boulders were pieces of suspicious looking concrete.

Correspondence with the OS has left us a little wiser, but not a lot. "When Triangulation Pillars," they said, "suffer extensive damage from vandals or extreme weather conditions, the pillar is converted to a surface block." The thought of a vandal equipped with a sledge-hammer, demolishing triangulation pillars is intriguing enough, but apparently the OS don't need the trig points any more. A Global Positioning System (ie. satellite) is replacing the friendly concrete columns, so how long will it be before a preservation order is slapped on the last remaining one? Visit them all before it is too late!

The sad demise of Cadair Bronwen North-east Top, demoted after a survey by John Barnard and Graham Jackson, has shortened this walk and Cadair Bronwen is now visted on Walk 7.2. In August 2007 a wake was held on the top in suitably appalling conditions. John gave a reading from the book "This top does not look or feel like a summit." And Eryl Selly read his poem:

Ode to Cadair Bronwen NE Top 1989 to 2007
Some of us always thought you were
An insignificant bump
But for a few years you shone with the glory
Of being a Nuttall
Now, once more, you are nothing
At all
So it was with sadness that we climbed a mountain
But descended a hill.

ROUTE DESCRIPTION

MOEL FFERNA

Take the lane beside the Blue Lion Hotel in the centre of Cynwyd which leads up towards the Berwyns. A pleasant alternative to the road walking is to turn right after quarter of a mile to visit the waterfalls. A track leads down to the old mill where a bridge beyond the house is crossed. The waterfalls are now straight ahead. Climb beside them on a faint path to reach a stile at the top of the woods. Cross this and go left (no stile) to descend to a bridge. The road is then rejoined at a footpath sign and soon enters the Cynwyd forest where there is an attractive lake hidden in the trees to the right. This is a reservoir which provides Cynwyd with water and in the past supplied a hydroelectric plant which generated power for the village. Half a mile into the forest at a boarded-up bungalow, Celyn Coed Isaf, fork right keeping on the tarmac road. Follow the forest edge to an open area where you pass below an occupied bungalow and then re-enter the forest. After about ¼ mile fork left uphill and climb south-east until a gate leads onto open heather moor. Following the original line of the ancient trackway, Ffordd Saeson, continue east rising gently to reach Bwlch Cynwyd to the south of Moel Fferna. It is possible to turn off the track before the bwlch and make a direct approach to Moel Fferna, but the heather is deep and difficult. It is easier to continue to the bwlch and then turn left beside the fence, where a narrow path leads up, crossing another fence, to the top. The heathery summit, now minus its trig point, has a very neat windshelter. To the south stretches the Berwyn ridge and to the north-east are the hills above Llangollen.

PEN BWLCH LLANDRILLO TOP *(Head of the Llandrillo Pass)*

The next summit lies about three miles to the south-west over rough, tough heather moor. Fortunately a path has developed beside the fence which runs the whole way, making walking and route-finding quite straightforward. The old fence posts, now disused, are made of flat stones with six holes drilled in them. It must have been quite a job threading three miles of wire through the holes! Retrace your steps from Moel Fferna to the col and follow the path beside the fence. This cannot be described as an exciting part of the walk, but the hills are very empty, the views extensive over cotton grass, bilberry and heather and like all wild country attractive because it is remote. Shortly after passing an infant forest, the summit is reached, a small cairn on a rocky outcrop just the other side of the fence. The top, which is surrounded by a sea of beautiful mosses of different colours and varieties, gives views of Moel Fferna and the Berwyn ridge.

Descend due south to Bwlch Llandrillo which is crossed by the line of an ancient trackway. Beside the track is the Wayfarer's Memorial. Here you turn right and after half a mile there is a signpost at a three-way junction. Pointing west to Llandrillo and east to Llanarmon DC the north-west fork for the return to Cynwyd is unsigned. The gated road has panoramic views of the Arans and the valley of the Afon Dyfrdwy, River Dee. After two miles fork right by a barn through a gate onto an old track. A mile further on, after it has become metalled, turn right again onto a narrow gated lane which leads back to Cynwyd.

Stone Circle below Cadair Bronwen

WALK 7.2 CADAIR BERWYN

SUMMITS:	Mynydd Tarw	2234ft (681m)
	Foel Wen South Top	2254ft (687m)
	Foel Wen	2267ft (691m)
	Tomle	2434ft (742m)
	Cadair Bronwen	2575ft (785m)
	Cadair Berwyn	2713ft (827m)
	Cadair Berwyn New Top	2723ft (830m)
	Moel Sych	2713ft (827m)
	Moel yr Ewig	2280ft (695m)
	Godor North Top	2215ft (675m)
	Godor	2228ft (679m)

DISTANCE: 10¹/₂ miles

ASCENT: 2650 feet

MAPS: OS Landranger sheet 125, Explorer 255

STARTING
POINT: (125-118308) Cwm Maen Gwynedd, 3 miles north of Llanrhaeadr-ym-Mochnant. Parking is very restricted. A car or two can be parked by the phone box and by the bridge over the stream.

Craig Berwyn

This is by far the best walk in the Berwyns. The usually ubiquitous Berwyn heather is largely absent on these hills and not only are these the highest mountains, but also the shaley eastern cliffs of Moel Sych and Craig Berwyn are a very dramatic contrast to the rolling moorland elsewhere in the range. In all a total of eleven summits are visited.

Although Cadair Berwyn looks much the grander mountain, it was given on first series maps as 2712ft and has always had to play second fiddle to Moel Sych which had the distinction of overtopping it by 1ft. Metrication and the Landranger series apparently levelled the score with both recorded at 827m, but Berwyn mountains don't give up easily. Careful examination of the 1:10,000 maps of the latest survey and subsequent confirmation from the OS, has established a completely new top. The new top is given a height of 830m, outclassing both previous contenders by at least 10ft. It is only quarter of a mile south of Cadair Berwyn and the fine rocky summit, much the best in the Berwyns, looks down on Llyn Lluncaws nearly 700ft below. Many thousands must have looked at this top remarking that it appeared higher, but it is only now that it emerges from obscurity to take the crown as the highest summit in the whole of the Berwyns.

Llanarmon Dyffryn Ceiriog to the east is a lovely little village with a church, school, post office and two pubs. Considering the facilities provided, there are surprisingly few houses. Llanrhaeadr-ym-Mochnant further south is a small attractive town famed as the home of William Morgan, who was responsible for the first translation of the Bible into Welsh. He was rector here for 23 years from 1572, afterwards being made Bishop of Llandaf and then Bishop of St Asaph. The Bible was published in 1588, only 50 years after Henry VIII had banned the official use of Welsh. In April 1988 the town celebrated the 400th anniversary of the first publication.

ROUTE DESCRIPTION

MYNYDD TARW *(Bull Mountain)*

Walk up the lane by the telephone box and then through Maes farmyard to the bend. The fields, which have huge piles of stones heaped up on them from the cleared land, are crossed by a public right of way which leads up to the corner of the wood. Keep by the edge of the wood, where a steady climb over short grass leads directly to the summit. The trees diminish in stature as height is gained until they fail altogether on the exposed top with sorry stunted growths. The summit, at the corner of the wood, is marked by a large stone windshelter fashioned from an ancient cairn. There are extensive views over to Cheshire and Shropshire.

FOEL WEN SOUTH TOP

Follow the fence north-west towards the Berwyn ridge of which there is an excellent view from here. Descend over a sharp little rock crest to the col, and then climb up gradually to the highest point, which is an unmarked spot to the left of the fence on otherwise featureless moorland.

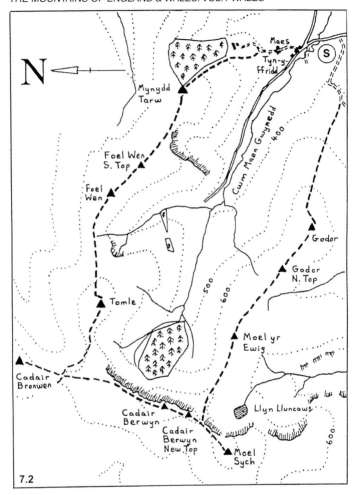

7.2

FOEL WEN *(White Bare Hill)*
Descending to the col between the two tops a short pull up then leads to the flat summit. The highest point is unmarked and somewhere on the featureless grass on the far side of the fence.

Cloudberry

TOMLE *(The Mire)*
It is an easy descent to the col beyond and then a steady plod up the fence for about half a mile to where the fence does a smart left turn to hit the top. A small cairn of white quartz on the short grass by the fence corner marks the summit.

CADAIR BRONWEN *(Bronwen's Chair)*
It is an easy descent to the col where an 8ft prehistoric standing stone acts as a guide post. Now turn right and follow Ffordd Gam Elin, Helen's crooked road which is said to be Roman and named after Elen, a Welsh princess who married a Roman emperor. Cresting the ridge you turn right and follow the path up to the impressive beehive summit cairn. From this legendary seat of Arthur there are good views of Cadair Berwyn, Moel Sych and the Rhinogs. The cloudberry can be found growing on this summit and this part of the Berwyns is the only place in Wales where it can be found. Its Welsh name is mwyar Berwyn, Berwyn berries. It is very like a blackberry, the white flowers have five petals and the composite fruit is orange when ripe.

CADAIR BERWYN *(Berwyn's Chair)*
Retrace your steps down the ridge then keep straight on and follow the fence up keeping close to the edge of the shattered cliffs of Craig Berwyn, it is a lovely airy walk along to the summit. The top has a concrete OS trig point surmounting an ancient cairn which is now also nearly obscured by grass. The views are extensive with the Rhinogs, Arans and Arenigs, and in the distance the mountains of northern Snowdonia.

Cadair Berwyn New Top from Cadair Berwyn

CADAIR BERWYN NEW TOP
Follow the fence, passing a huge windshelter constructed from an ancient cairn, to this the highest summit in the Berwyns. It is much more dramatic than its neighbours and a far more fitting top for a mountain with its jagged rocks and a steep drop to the forest below which fills the head of the cwm.

MOEL SYCH *(Dry Bare Hill)*
It is a pleasant stroll over grass to the left of the fence to this next top, now only the second highest of the Berwyns. The summit, which is the far side of a three-fence junction, has a large cairn and is claimed to be the best viewpoint in Wales. On a clear day the distant views include the full length of the Carneddau, Tryfan and the Glyders, Snowdon, Cnicht and the Moelwyns, the Arenigs, Rhinogs and, of course, the Arans.

MOEL YR EWIG *(Bare Hill of the Hind)*
Retrace your steps towards Cadair Berwyn to the col, where as the ground begins to rise again, a small path down a gully leads to the fence on the south-east ridge high above Llyn Lluncaws, cheese-shaped lake. Walk along the ridge, past a couple of subsidiary bumps, using the fence as a guide in mist to the Moel yr Ewig top, which is a grassy hill. The highest point is the second grassy mound to the left of the fence. There is no cairn.

GODOR NORTH-WEST TOP
The next summit is about half a mile away. Continue along the line of the fence

and where it makes a detour to the right, cut straight across the rough open moor to rejoin it further on. This is hard going over tussocky grass and rather boggy, but it is the only uncomfortable bit encountered on this walk and the going improves as the summit is approached. The highest point is unmarked and is just before a fence comes in from the left.

GODOR *(Break)*

Continue along the fence for another half mile and just before a three-fence junction, a small white cairn on the left marks the highest point on tussocky grass.

The tenth and last top now completed, descend the east ridge to pick up the right of way near Bryn-gwyn. This leads out to the lane where you turn left to return to Tyn y ffridd.

WALK 7.3 POST GWYN

SUMMITS:	Post Gwyn	2182ft (665m)
DISTANCE:	5½ miles	
ASCENT:	1200 feet	
MAPS:	OS Landranger sheet 125, Explorer 255	
STARTING POINT:	(125-073295) Pistyll Rhaeadr at the end of the minor road 4 miles north-west of Llanrhaeadr-ym-Mochnant. Car park and toilets.	

Post Gwyn, south-west of the main Berwyn ridge, is set in a sea of heather and tussocky moorland which firmly deters an approach from the north and it is not visited very often, certainly not from this side. Determined to collect this top, we stumbled on vowing never again, until we had ticked it off. Descending quickly to the Afon Disgynfa, the valley raised a question mark against our intentions. It was grassy, easy walking and came down to a stupendous waterfall. Perhaps it was worth a second look.

The approach from the east is different. Despite the undoubted popularity of Pistyll Rhaeadr, the road up the valley is surprisingly narrow, only wide enough in some places for one car, but at the valley head is the biggest waterfall in Wales. Pistyll Rhaeadr, 240ft in height, has at its foot the pleasant farmhouse of Tan-y-pistyll visited by George Borrow, where he had a drink of buttermilk. It became ruined, but was rebuilt about 20 years ago, so now you can have tea and scones and watch the falls in comfort. This is of course as far as the average visitor goes, though a few brave the steep ascent to the top of the falls, but beyond the valley is quiet and peaceful.

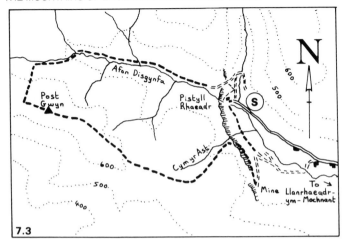

7.3

It was not always so, as the remains of the lead mines a mile down the valley testify. These were worked in the late nineteenth century, but without great financial success. A leat was constructed to channel water from the falls all the way to the mine where it was used in separating the ore by washing. A slate quarry, high on the cliffs away to the left of the falls opened later, but was likewise unsuccessful as the slate beds were not of the fine quality found in such places as Blaenau Ffestiniog. The gigantic blocks in the valley are however nothing to do with the quarry and were broken from the cliffs above by glacial action.

ROUTE DESCRIPTION

POST GWYN *(White Pillar)*

A gate beside the farm is signposted as a public footpath and this is followed towards the falls. By the bridge spanning the stream, the path goes right through beech trees, to a small gate to join a track just beyond the next gate. A well constructed stepped footpath is signed left off the track and up the steep slopes, skirting the falls hidden in the trees to the left. A rough track is joined and then followed left above the falls where a waymark indicates left to view the top of the falls, but the route to the hills continues up the valley on a clear grassy path which is very easy walking.

After a mile the valley of Cwm Rhiwiau on the right leads up towards Moel Sych. Stay by the Afon Disgynfa although the path begins to fade out. The next valley on the right is Cwm yr Eithin, valley of the gorse, and easier going will then be found on the left side of the stream up Blaen Glaswen. This wide glacial valley is usually very quiet and you will probably have it completely to yourself.

On reaching the reedy area, keep above this and then turn left up a shallow dip in the slope which leads to the ridge. The sheep use this route and it is a good one, bringing you easily to the ridge and avoiding the heather. Turn left and it is only a short way over the rather boggy and heathery moor with the occasional bit of easy grass to the top. When reached this turns out to be grassy, with a rocky outcrop on which is built the cairn of tumbled stones. On the other side of the valley Moel Sych is prominent.

Heading now south-east, Cadair Berwyn comes into view. Keep to the left side of the broad ridge in order to avoid the more difficult moorland walking until a flat col is reached in a little over a mile. Skirting the next minor top on its left, descend on the right of Cwm yr Ast staying fairly high again to remain on the grass until a gateway is reached above Craig y Mŵn, crag of the ore, where just to the left, the stream throws itself over the edge.

Before descending the path which goes right through a gateway, cunningly finding an easy but exposed way down the cliff, an airy promontory gives an excellent bird's-eye view of the valley with Pistyll Rhaeadr at its head.

The path slants gradually down until, after half a mile the old lead mine workings are reached. Zigzag down the mine track and then follow the line of the old leat which channelled water to the mine from the falls. Ignoring the waymark which points over a stile down into the valley, continue along the channel and just after crossing a stream, there is the only remaining bit of stone walling of the original leat.

On entering the trees Pistyll Rhaeadr appears directly ahead and close by are the remains of the ramp serving the old slate quarry. Go on to the very end of the leat for the best view of the falls and then descend to cross the river at the bridge.

WALK 7.4 FOEL CWM SIAN LLŴYD

SUMMITS:	Foel Cwm Sian Llŵyd 2126ft (648m)
DISTANCE:	2 miles
ASCENT:	600 feet
MAPS:	OS Landranger sheet 125, Explorer 255
STARTING POINT:	(125-006321) The Milltir Gerrig Pass, 5 miles north of Llangynog on the B4391. Ample parking beside the road.

After the spectacular, almost alpine, approach up the Milltir Gerrig Pass from

Llangynog, Foel Cwm Sian Llŵyd looks a very boring mountain indeed. Its rough, heather slopes are not encouraging and only the dedicated peak-bagger will be tempted to explore further. But the ascent is not nearly as bad as it looks; an old, overgrown track sets you well on the way and the heather is (for Berwyn heather) very easy to walk through. Your reward is an unexpected, but truly magnificent view and a large number of the 2000ft summits in North Wales can be identified from here.

Milltir Gerrig just means milestone. An old road crossed the pass here at a height of 1595ft and made its way down to Bala. Llangynog, at the foot of the pass was a harp-making centre. It is an attractive old mining village at the junction of two valleys. In the first half of the eighteenth century lead from here was taken to be smelted at Welshpool. The smeltery was on the navigable River Severn at Pool Quay.

A couple of miles to the west of the village and only three miles south-east of the summit of Foel Cwm Sian Llŵyd, is the hamlet of Pennant Melangell. Here in the twelfth century, legend tells that Sister Melangell who lived here as a hermit, sheltered a hunted hare under her skirts. The prince leading the hunt was so impressed he gave her some land on which to build an abbey. The present church is of Celtic origin and is set in a large circular churchyard with a stone lychgate. It possesses a fifteenth-century rood-screen depicting scenes from the legend and a reconstructed twelfth-century shrine.

ROUTE DESCRIPTION

FOEL CWM SIAN LLŴYD *(Bare Hill of Grey Jane's Valley)*

A faint path leads through heather on the left of the stream, though there is now little sign of the ruined cottage in the illustration. When the path peters out continue in the same direction, taking sheep trods that keep to the little

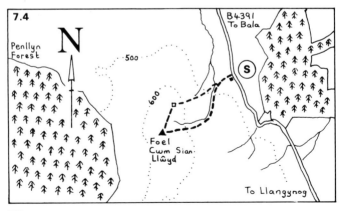

Ruined cottage below Foel Cwm Sian Llŵyd

gullies and follow the line of the stream all the way to the flat, heathery top. Bear left to the OS trig point which is a magnificent viewpoint. From here you can see for miles, the Berwyn ridge stretches out to either side and most of its 2000ft summits can be easily identified. The Aran ridge is silhouetted against the sky to the south-west and the Rhinogs, Arenigs and the high mountains of Snowdonia are all spread out in a superb panorama.

Traverse the somewhat peaty summit plateau north-east to a ruined building, which on closer inspection proves to have been constructed from and upon an ancient cairn. Pathless heather which is a struggle in ascent, is much easier going down and a direct line can be taken back to the start with Cadair Bronwen in the distance indicating the direction.

WALK 7.5 THE WESTERN BERWYNS

SUMMITS:	Foel Goch	2011ft (613m)
	Trum y Gwragedd	2008ft (612m)
	Foel y Geifr	2054ft (626m)
	Pen y Boncyn Trefeilw	2119ft (646m)
	Stac Rhos	2067ft (630m)
	Cefn Gwyntog	2018ft (615m)
	Cyrniau Nod	2188ft (667m)
	Y Groes Fagl	2162ft (659m)

DISTANCE: 11½ miles

ASCENT: 2300 feet

MAPS: OS Landranger sheet 125
Explorer OL23 - Cadair Idris & Llyn Tegid and Explorer 255

STARTING
POINT: (125-952300) The foot of the Hirnant Pass, 5 miles south-east of Bala. Roadside parking.

The western Berwyns above the Penllyn Forest are covered in deep, strength-sapping heather which defends them vigorously and deters most walkers. These mountains are rarely visited save by the peak-bagger as there are few features of interest, but the first three tops to the west of the Hirnant Pass are pleasant enough, with their steep easterly slopes dropping straight down to the narrow little road from Bala to Lake Vyrnwy.

It is the summits to the east of the pass that more correctly deserve the title of Boring Berwyns, though the walk can be enlivened by deciphering the occasional boundary stone. These heathery lumps would be very remote and isolated were it not for the Forestry Commission road that ambles along the ridge. Using this as a base from which to make forays into the heathery jungle, the remaining five tops can be visited with comparative ease.

One starts the walk feeling the hills have been spoilt by the bulldozed track; it is merely an acquaintance used because it is there. But after one or two expeditions have been made from it to the more remote summits, it attains the character of an old friend and is joined for the last time with some relief. Cefn Gwyntog is a new summit not shown on the old OS maps, the surveyors, totally defeated by the heather never got that far.

One sunny May weekend, Bwlch y Groes-fagl, the pass between Cyrniau Nod and Y Groes Fagl, had been taken over. Closer investigation revealed six tall radio masts and several army vehicles and tents, all neatly camouflaged. But all was deserted, it was like the *Marie Celeste*. Sleeping bags, food and gear all lay about as if abandoned hurriedly or overwhelmed in some

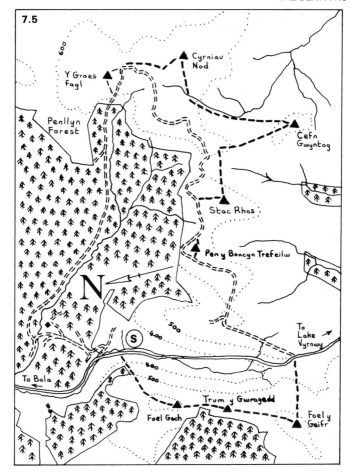

catastrophe. Eventually we traced a strange roaring noise to one tightly zipped tent. It was a very hot day and inside were several hot soldiers. "We're on operations," they said. "We've been stood down," they said. "We're watching the Cup Final."

ROUTE DESCRIPTION

FOEL GOCH *(Red Bare Hill)*
Aiming for the end of the forest which fringes the northern ridge of Foel Goch, climb steep grassy slopes to a faint path which follows the fence at the forest edge up through heather and bilberry. When the angle eases, the going underfoot becomes rougher till the ridge is reached where the fence turns sharply right and Bala Lake can be seen ahead. The summit is about quarter of a mile to the south along the broad heathery ridge. The highest point on the flat top of heather and grass is marked by a few slaty rocks.

TRUM Y GWRAGEDD *(Ridge of the Wives)*
Continue along the ridge to the south, keeping to the left where the ground drops steeply away to Cwm Hirnant. The going is now much easier and a faint track can be followed which curves round to join the fence crossing the summit. The highest point, a grassy and heathery top, is unmarked and just on the other side of the fence. The name of this summit has been wrongly spelt by the OS.

FOEL Y GEIFR *(Bare Hill of the Goats)*
The faint track continues to the next summit, a mile away, with the forest below to the right. The fence provides a good guide in misty conditions. The OS trig point, attractively covered in lichen, is a short way from where the fence kinks right, situated on the top of an ancient cairn surrounded by a few white stones. The Aran mountains lie to the west, but this viewpoint does not do them justice, as they appear strangely diminished from here. The rest of the Berwyn ridge can be seen stretching away to the east.

PEN Y BONCYN TREFEILW *(Top of the Hillock)*
The walk continues by crossing the Hirnant Pass road at the col. It is a rough descent over heather and then grass to the road. From the summit of the pass a bulldozed track climbs gently to the next summit and then meanders along the ridge. These tracks can be found throughout the mountains of Wales, although scorned by the purists, they are much appreciated by the less hardy after a few miles of pathless heather bashing. After about a mile and half, a fence divides the rough moorland from a grassy field and the track runs north-east parallel to this along the summit ridge. The highest point in the field at the far end of the ridge was once marked by a boundary stone inscribed DP, but this is reported to have vanished.

STAC RHOS *(Moor Stack)*
Return to the track; after about half a mile a gate on the right gives access to the next summit which can easily be reached over grass, keeping to the left of the heather. The summit area has seven separate contour rings at 630m

in close proximity to one another, none of which has been singled out by the OS. However, after much careful on the spot survey work, the north-east most ring appears to be fractionally higher.

CEFN GWYNTOG *(Windy Ridge)*

Follow the fence east for half a mile, first down the field and then across a rather boggy section where the ivy-leaved crowfoot flowers. A boundary stone with HB 1852 on one side and DP on the other, marks the spot where a subsidiary ridge leads south to the next top. A very rough half mile over heather with no trace of path must be negotiated to gain the summit which is unfortunately at the far end of the ridge. It is the last bump to be reached and is marked by an upright stone.

CYRNIAU NOD *(Mark Cairns)*

Returning northwards, descend gradually to join the stream of Nant Cyrniau Nod, which can be followed most of the way to the next summit. This proves somewhat easier going than a direct ascent through the heather. A fence crosses the top and the heather and grassy summit is on the other side, marked by a substantial cairn. Surrounded by extensive heather moorland, this summit looks and feels a long way from anywhere. To the north-east lie Cadair Berwyn and Moel Sych.

Y GROES FAGL *(Snare's Cross)*

Keep by the fence going north-west to a fence junction, then follow this right to rejoin the track for a few yards. Where the track bends left, take a small path which continues in the same direction to the final summit where, after 50ft of ascent, the flat, heathery top is marked by a 6ft post.

Rejoin the track for the last time and follow it downhill through the forest for a couple of miles. Turn left past Ystrad-y-groes, a cottage in a clearing. Keep to the main forest road, ignoring the minor tracks to either side, and climb to the col where you fork left to leave the wood. From here it is a short distance downhill to the Hirnant Pass.

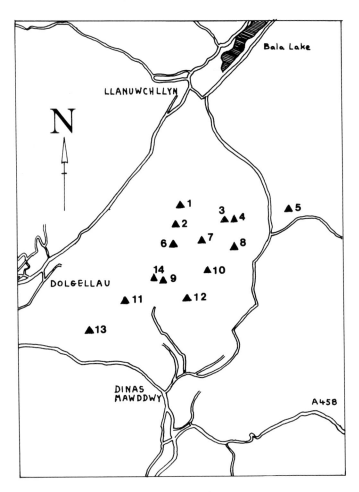

8. THE ARANS

CHAPTER 8: THE ARANS

TOP	NAME	HEIGHT	GRID REF	WALK No.
1	Aran Benllyn	885m	125-867243 SH	8.1
2	Erw y Ddafad-ddu	872m	125-865234 SH	8.1
3	Esgeiriau Gwynion	671m	125-890236 SH	8.2
4	Foel Rhudd	659m	125-896240 SH	8.2
5	Moel y Cerrig Duon	625m	125-923241 SH	8.2
6	Aran Fawddwy	905m	125-863224 SH	8.1
7	Foel Hafod-fynydd	689m	125-877227 SH	8.2
8	Llechwedd Du	614m	125-894224 SH	8.2
9	Gwaun y Llwyni	685m	125-857205 SH	8.1
10	Gwaun Lydan	632m	125-880212 SH	8.1
11	Glasgwm	780m	125-837195 SH	8.3
12	Pen yr Allt Uchaf	620m	125-871197 SH	8.1
13	Pen y Bryn-fforchog	685m	125-818179 SH	8.3
14	Waun Camddwr	621m	125-848206 SH	8.1

Looking to Aran Benllyn from Aran Fawddwy

131

The Arans from Bala Lake

WALK 8.1 THE ARAN RIDGE

SUMMITS:	Pen y Allt Uchaf	2034ft (620m)
	Gwaun Lydan	2073ft (632m)
	Aran Fawddwy	2969ft (905m)
	Erw y Ddafad-ddu	2861ft (872m)
	Aran Benllyn	2904ft (885m)
	Gwaun y Llwyni	2247ft (685m)
	Waun Camddwr	2037ft (621m)

DISTANCE: 11¹/₂ miles

ASCENT: 3400 feet

MAPS: OS Landranger sheet 125
Explorer OL23 - Cadair Idris & Llyn Tegid

STARTING
POINT: (125-854185) The end of the minor road in Cwm Cywarch 3
miles north of Dinas Mawddwy. Cars may be parked at the far
end of the open land beside the road.

The principal summits of the Arans stretch in a long high level ridge from Llanuwchllyn, at the southern end of Bala Lake, for a distance of about 8 miles to the village of Dinas Mawddwy in the Dovey valley. Although looking impressive from Bala Lake, Llyn Tegid the largest natural lake in Wales, the finest aspect of these hills is the almost continuous 6-mile stretch of cliffs which flank the eastern side of the ridge. At the southern end are the brooding cliffs of Craig Cywarch while beneath the shattered rocks of Aran Fawddwy is Creiglyn Dyfi, the source of the River Dyfi or Dovey. Aran Fawddwy is the highest mountain in Wales to the south of Snowdon and if it were only 31ft higher it would join the ranks of the 3000ft summits. This though would no doubt upset attempts on the 3000ft peaks as Snowdon is some 25 miles to the north.

Since publication of the first edition of this book the access situation on the Arans has improved significantly. The only problem is that hardly anyone knows about it! Under the Tir Cymen scheme, managed by the Countryside Council for Wales, access is now allowed over much of the high land in this area. But how do you know where you are entitled to go? The answer is that detailed maps can be consulted at all the Tourist Information Centres and Snowdonia National Park Information Centres. Be persistent though, some centres don't even know they've got them.

While Tir Cymen is restricted in extent, a new scheme Tir Gofal has just been launched, which applies to the whole of Wales.

Dinas Mawddwy, to the south of the Arans is a pleasant little Welsh-speaking village. In the sixteenth century it was the headquarters of the

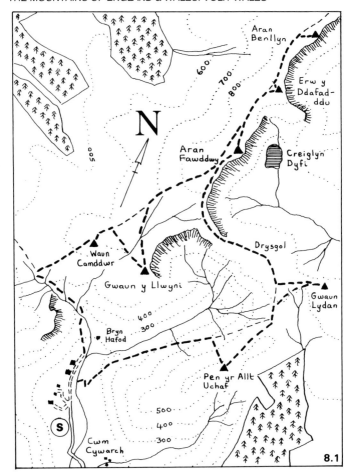

Gwylliad Cochion, a group of red-haired robbers who were finally caught and executed in 1555. George Borrow passed through Dinas Mawddwy on his walking tour of Wales, his book *Wild Wales* published in 1862 was most uncomplimentary.

'Dinas, though at one time a place of considerable importance, if we may judge from its name which signifies a fortified city, is at present little more than a collection of filthy huts. But though a dirty squalid place, I found it anything but silent and deserted. Fierce-looking red-haired men, who seemed as if they might be descendants of the red-haired banditti of old, were staggering about, and sounds of drunken revelry echoed from the huts. I subsequently learned that Dinas was the headquarters of miners, the neighbourhood abounding with mines of both lead and stone. I was glad to leave it behind me.'

Dinas Mawddwy has improved considerably since those times and is now a tourist centre with a good pub, hotels and even a working woollen mill. At one time it was quite industrial with its mines and quarries, but now there is only the sheep farming and forestry.

After an easy approach up the old peat-cutting track of Hengwm and detours to minor peaks, the main ridge is gained via Drysgol, an airy viewpoint, but with insufficient elevation on its west side to be a separate summit. Its memorial cairn was built by members of the RAF St Athan Mountain Rescue Team to Mike Aspain, who in June 1960, was killed by lightning near this spot whilst on duty with the team. He was only 18.

The whole of the main ridge is above 2500ft and because of the altitude, conditions on the tops in winter can be arctic, with few walkers to produce the well trampled paths of the more popular summits. While you are up there keep an eye open for Noah's Ark, legend has it that this is where the Flood began and the Ark was deposited on the Aran ridge when the waters went down.

ROUTE DESCRIPTION

PEN YR ALLT UCHAF *(Top of the Highest Hillside)*
Walk down the tarmac road for a few yards to the footbridge and ford and turn right, signposted Arans. The track leads up a sunken lane overhung with hawthorn trees to the open hillside. Continue to climb steadily on this old path up the Hengwm valley, with the Mountain Club climbing hut beneath the cliffs opposite. After one and a half miles at a ladder stile above the head of the valley, turn right up the fence which leads over very steep rough grass straight to this minor summit, really only a high point on the ridge. The highest point, which is grassy with no cairn, is on the far side of the ridge fence. There are extensive views in all directions with Aran Fawddwy dominating the scene ahead.

GWAUN LYDAN *(Broad Moor)*
Aim north to the foot of the ridge leading to Drysgol, keeping close to the edge of the drop into Hengwm to avoid the peat hags. From the col go north round the headwaters of Pumryd Fawr, where the full extent of the Aran ridge comes into view with Creiglyn Dyfi at the foot of the cliffs. Follow the fence east to find the highest point just to its north on the moor of tussocky grass. There is no cairn, but this is a marvellous viewpoint and for such a small hill the views are

Aran Fawddwy from Drysgol

quite outstanding, stretching far to the east and way beyond Glasgwm to the south-west.

ARAN FAWDDWY *(Mawddwy Mountain)*
Return to the col and follow the permissive path up Drysgol climbing to the memorial cairn perched on the edge of the drop. From here the concessionary path crosses the fence and climbs by a well cairned route on a direct line to the summit ridge. From a prominent cairn at the end of the ridge it is about a quarter mile to the summit. This, the highest of the Arans, is marked by a stone OS trig point set on a huge pile of boulders on the edge of a dizzy drop to Creiglyn Dyfi. The views are extensive with Pumlumon away to the south, westwards Cadair Idris, the Rhinogs and the sea, while north-west is Snowdon. Ahead the ridge stretches northwards towards Bala Lake and the Arenigs.

ERW Y DDAFAD-DDU *(Acre of the Black Sheep)*
After descending northwards steeply over boulders to a ladder stile at the col it is an easy half mile stroll to the next summit where a broad grassy sweep drops down to Creiglyn Dyfi. A cairn stands on the top, high above the lake midway between the grander heights of Aran Fawddwy and Aran Benllyn.

ARAN BENLLYN *(Mountain at the Head of the Lake)*
Continue north for another half mile crossing over two more stiles; the second one is just below the summit whose north side is veined with quartz. There is a rough untidy cairn to the north of a ruined wall where there are good views of tiny Llyn Pen Aran high on the ridge with Bala Lake in the valley beyond, but the highest point, the OS spot height, is on the south side of the wall on the edge of the cliffs.

GWAUN Y LLWYNI *(Moorland of the Bushes)*
Return along the ridge, this time keeping to the right of the high ground of the summits but crossing the same ladder stiles. A ruined fence comes up from the valley on the right to join a new fence below the prominent cairn on the end of the Aran Fawddwy ridge. Follow the concession path south-west to the left of the fence, crossing a ladder stile and continuing in the same direction descending steeply. When the ground levels off by a rocky tor, head south-east over rough grass, past the site of an air crash, crossing to the eastern edge with a view into Hengwm below. Follow the ridge up to the summit of Gwaun y Llwyni, whose top is crossed by an old fence with just a few pieces of slate marking the highest point.

WAUN CAMDDWR *(Moor of the Crooked Stream)*
Head down north-west along the line of the old fence to rejoin the path which is boggy in places, but helpful planks of wood cross the worst bits. Follow the fence left to this new top, which is on the left, just before the next fence junction. Nagged by Myrddyn to go and have another look at this summit, we found the rocky knoll rises by 16m, though the OS have overlooked it and omitted an encircling 620m contour.

At the col turn left and following the waymarks descend the delightful little path beside the waterfalls back to Cwm Cywarch.

WALK 8.2 THE EASTERN ARANS

SUMMITS:		
	Llechwedd Du	2014ft (614m)
	Foel Rhudd	2162ft (659m)
	Esgeiriau Gwynion	2201ft (671m)
	Foel Hafod-fynydd	2260ft (689m)
	Moel y Cerrig Duon	2051ft (625m)

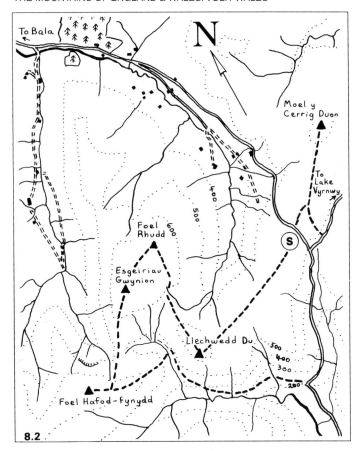

8.2

DISTANCE: 9½ miles

ASCENT: 2700 feet

MAPS: OS Landranger sheet 125
Explorer OL23 - Cadair Idris & Llyn Tegid

STARTING
POINT: (125-913233) Bwlch y Groes. The summit of the minor road
from Llanuwchllyn to Dinas Mawddy. Car park.

These eastern summits of windswept moorland are pleasant enough, but no rivals to the rocky crest of the main Aran ridge. However they are a good vantage point for the eastern facing cliffs of Aran Fawddwy and Aran Benllyn and few if any people are likely to be met on their grassy slopes. On reaching Foel Hafod-fynydd the twin peaks of the main ridge beckon temptingly and Creiglyn Dyfi looks a delightful spot to linger.

After admiring the superb rock scenery of the cwm and the ridges you must return from whence you came. The return journey though has compensation in the lovely waterfalls at the head of the Afon Dyfi.

To the east is an extensive area of high wild moorland, but Moel y Cerrig Duon is the only 2000ft top. Beyond is the reservoir of Lake Vyrnwy, completed in 1892 to supply Liverpool with water. The village of Llanwddyn, which was flooded by the reservoir, has been rebuilt, complete with a church and a chapel, below the dam. The slopes around the lake have been forested which was originally done in order to stabilise them. With many deciduous trees planted along its margins the lakeside road is very attractive, while the tower of the valve house is straight out of a fairy tale.

ROUTE DESCRIPTION

LLECHWEDD DU *(Black Hillside)*
Follow the fence south-west from the car park at Bwlch y Groes, pass of the cross, keeping to its left-hand side. Although the moor is rough and boggy, our only visits have been in winter when the ground was hard frozen and so cold one Christmas that the orange squash froze in the rucksack. In these conditions the bogs present no problems. After one and a half miles, when the fence turns north, continue in the same direction for 100 yards to a small cairn of white quartz on the grassy top. On a good seeing day there is a wide panorama to the north, east and south, but the most striking view is that to the west where the Aran ridge forms the skyline with the lowly Foel Hafod-fynydd crouching under the lee of the mountain range.

FOEL RHUDD *(Red Bare Hill)*
Returning to the fence, passing some weird mushroom-shaped peat hags, the going is now much easier underfoot. In half a mile at the bwlch, cross the fence and after following the Afon Twrch, hog river, upstream for a short way, aim north-east for the grassy summit which is marked by a wooden fence post wedged between a few white stones just before another fence. Ahead lies the Bala valley with the Arenigs beyond.

ESGEIRIAU GWYNION *(White Ridges)*
Follow the fence west and then south to a three-way junction on the summit of Esgeiriau Gwynion. The highest point on the tussocky moor is crossed by the south-west branch before it descends steeply into the valley. The western

slopes of this mountain are streaked with the white quartz from which it gets its name.

FOEL HAFOD-FYNYDD *(Bare Hill of the Mountain Summer Dwelling)*

Descend to Bwlch Sirddyn following the fence first south-west and then south to cross the right of way to Cwm Croes, valley of the cross. The fence continues up Foel Hafod-fynydd and although the way looks very steep it is deceptive and only 400ft of ascent to the ridge. Turn right for an easy half mile along the fence to the summit, which is the second and slightly higher bump on the ridge; both tops are marked by cairns. The view of the rocky cliffs and Craiglyn Dyfi below is magnificent and the continuation up the grassy sweep to the main ridge of the Arans tempting.

MOEL Y CERRIG DUON *(Bare Hill of the Black Stones)*

Return east along the ridge, veering left from the fence near the head of the valley to avoid the deep ravine of Ceunant y Briddell. Cross the stream to join the right of way which follows the line of a bulldozed track which, badly eroded, zigzags down past the ravine with its waterfalls. At the foot of the ravine the stream tumbles down to join the Llaethnant, milk stream, becoming the infant Afon Dyfi or River Dovey. Next, in the space of quarter of a mile the river drops 500ft in a series of magnificent waterfalls and pools. One of these forms a natural swimming pool complete with deep end and shallow end. The old right of way has disappeared, but the track continues to Blaen-pennant where a footpath bypasses the farm to rejoin the track just before it emerges onto the road at the hairpin bend. The quiet gated road climbs steadily, passing a rock slab inscribed with the date of 1796 RW. In just over a mile turn right towards Llanwddyn and Lake Vyrnwy whose Welsh name is Llyn Efyrnwy. After 200 yards a notice welcomes you to Montgomeryshire; Croeso Maldwyn. Turn left here and follow yet another fence up to the skyline where there is what appears to be a television aerial sporting a solar panel. This is a global seismology station. Moel y Cerrig Duon must have hidden subterranean attractions, as a research group came here all the way from Edinburgh to put it up! Follow the fence north-east for a further half mile, crossing to the other side at a hurdle at the low point. The top is marked by a cairn on the rough moor just to the left of the fence. Lake Vyrnwy can be glimpsed to the east framed by the V-shape of the Eunant valley.

The return is less than a mile of easy walking keeping to the north of the fence which leads straight back to the road at Bwlch y Groes.

WALK 8.3 THE SOUTHERN ARANS

SUMMITS:	Glasgwm	2559ft (780m)
	Pen y Bryn-fforchog	2247ft (685m)
DISTANCE:	6¹/2 miles	
ASCENT:	2350 feet	
MAPS:	OS Landranger sheet 125	
	Explorer OL23 - Cadair Idris & Llyn Tegid	
STARTING POINT:	(125-854185) The end of the minor road in Cwm Cywarch, 3 miles north of Dinas Mawddwy. Cars may be parked at the far end of the open land beside the road.	

The southern summits of the Arans are not visited very often compared with the more dramatic heights of Aran Benllyn and Aran Fawddwy, but although less rugged than the ridge to the north they have a quiet beauty of their own. The summit of Glasgwm is quite unique as almost at the highest point is Llyn y Fign, the largest natural stretch of water to be found anywhere within a few yards of the cairn of a 2000ft mountain.

Pen y Bryn-fforchog is distinguished by its height and not much else. The rounded grassy summit is without even a cairn, but the descent through the forest makes a welcome change of scene, especially so if the weather is bad when the shelter afforded by the trees is a sudden contrast to the windswept tops. The zigzag track down to Cwm Cywarch, although an eyesore, gives an easy descent with beautiful views if the immediate foreground is ignored. This track is a bit of a mystery. Said to be for tending the sheep, it stops abruptly without so much as a gate through the fence onto the hillside. Many of the less frequented hills of Wales are regrettably scarred by such bulldozed tracks, some of which can be blamed on forestry, but all leading boldly uphill to stop in the middle of nowhere.

The southern Arans can be ascended from either the east or the west side of the ridge. To the west the slopes are gentle and grassy and though a good track leads up from Rhydymain, the alternative route from Cwm Cywarch is a much more dramatic and attractive ascent by little waterfalls which are at their best after (or during!) heavy rain. Strong walkers may prefer to link this walk with the end of Walk 8.1 to save the reascent, but this part of the walk, in whichever direction it is done, is one of the most attractive in this area.

ROUTE DESCRIPTION

GLASGWM *(Blue Valley)*
The tarmac road comes to an end in Cwm Cywarch and become a farm track. Carry straight on, ignoring the footbridge and ford to the right and passing

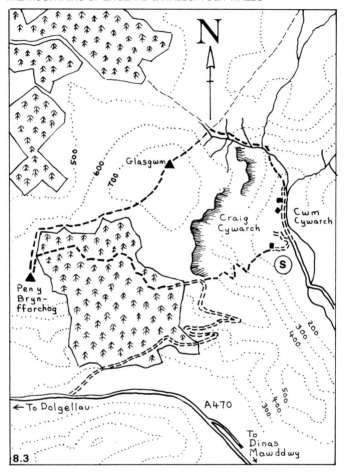

Blaencywarch Farm on the left to follow the footpath over a ladder stile at a gate. The route is clearly waymarked and soon turns left, signposted Rhydymain & Aran, over another ladder stile just below Bryn Hafod, a club hut belonging to the Mountain Club. This was opened in 1965 and in 1974 an equipped rescue hut was added. The path now starts to climb, passing on the right a glacier-smoothed outcrop. Above, on the left is Craig Cywarch, the

Bryn Hafod, Cwm Cywarch

most impressive cliff in the Arans, with many high standard rock climbs. The path is marked at frequent intervals with painted yellow arrows on the rocks. This is not a custom one would wish to encourage, but nevertheless after crossing a wooden bridge, the path zigzags through the rocks where their guidance is a useful indication of the best line to follow. Small tributary streams are crossed and higher up there are some attractive waterfalls where the stream is confined between rock walls in a steep-sided chasm. As the ascent eases, there is a ruin on the left and the fence is then followed up to the col where the concession path to the Aran ridge turns right at a small signpost. Carry straight on for a short way, passing a small lake, to where a fence comes down from the left. Cross the stile and turn left to follow the fence up the hillside for about half a mile until it turns abruptly right enclosing a small lake. The grassy summit with a rocky knoll is a few yards beyond the fence corner with a solidly built conical cairn. Seated by this, one looks down on a large and attractive expanse of water, Llyn y Fign, lake of the bog.

PEN Y BRYN-FFORCHOG *(Top of the Forked Hill)*
The fence provides an excellent guide to the next summit, and while the line can be straightened a little, in mist the fence is most reassuring. Trending generally south-west, it leads gently downhill to the forest whose edge should be followed west. When this turns south, follow a fence which diverges gradually from the trees and leads to the summit. The highest point is a few yards on the other side of the fence and just before the fence corner with a little tarn beyond. There is no cairn on the grassy top, but a few small pieces of slate indicate where people think it ought to be.

Return to the forest and locate a wide ride which starts near the forest corner. This goes east over rough grass for about three quarters of a mile to cross a stream then swings round to the south-east. Up to now there has been no difficulty in following the route in the forest as there hasn't been any alternative way through! Now, at the T-junction with a ride coming in from the right, turn left and soon the ride becomes a forest gravel track and then the edge of the wood is reached at a gate. The major track bends right shortly, but don't be tempted to follow it as this will lead you down the wrong side of the mountain. At the hairpin bend by the second gate, go left across the grass, where there are very faint signs of an old path and cross the fence (no stile although it is a public right of way). The hillside ahead is very steep indeed, but a narrow and rough forest track zigzags down the slope in a series of tight hairpin bends, making the descent easy and rapid. In places the track has been scoured away by storms and is now impassable to vehicles without further work. The scenery of the Cywarch cliffs on the left is very wild and impressive. As the valley floor is reached, the track leads past a farm to join the end of the road.

Above Cwm Cywarch

Rhinog Fach and ice on Llyn Hywel

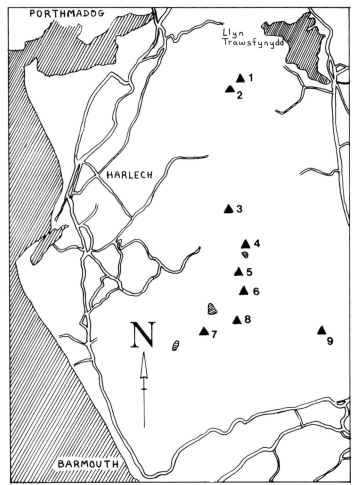

9. THE RHINOGS

CHAPTER 9: THE RHINOGS

TOP	NAME	HEIGHT	GRID REF	WALK No.
1	Foel Penolau	614m	124-662348 SH	9.2
2	Moel Ysgyfarnogod	623m	124-658346 SH	9.2
3	Rhinog Fawr	720m	124-657290 SH	9.1
4	Rhinog Fach	712m	124-665270 SH	9.1
5	Y Llethr	756m	124-661258 SH	9.1
6	Crib-y-rhiw	670m	124-664248 SH	9.1
7	Diffwys West Top	642m	124-648229 SH	9.1
8	Diffwys	750m	124-661234 SH	9.1
9	Y Garn	629m	124-703230 SH	9.3

Rhinog Fawr from the summit of Rhinog Fach

WALK 9.1 RHINOG FAWR AND RHINOG FACH

SUMMITS:	Rhinog Fawr	2362ft (720m)
	Rhinog Fach	2336ft (712m)
	Y Llethr	2480ft (756m)
	Crib-y-rhiw	2198ft (670m)
	Diffwys	2461ft (750m)
	Diffwys West Top	2106ft (642m)

DISTANCE: 11 miles

ASCENT: 4400 feet

MAPS: OS Landranger sheet 124
Explorer OL18 - Harlech, Porthmadog & Bala / Y Bala

STARTING
POINT: (124-642270) Cwm Nantcol at the end of a minor road south-east of Harlech. Cars may be parked for a small fee.

The northern Rhinogs present some of the roughest and toughest walking to be found anywhere in Wales and while Rhinog Fawr and Rhinog Fach belong firmly to the character of this area, with deep heather and ankle-twisting rocks, the hills southwards gradually relent until finally the grassy slopes of Diffwys are reached. Perhaps because of the difficult of approach and retreat, the tops of Rhinog Fawr and Rhinog Fach have the feel of much higher mountains and this remote wildness is especially strongly felt on days of low cloud and rain. The highest top is in fact Y Llethr, but it is the two Rhinogs which are the jewels.

Rhinog comes from the Welsh word rhiniog meaning threshold and these hills are indeed the threshold to the lands of Ardudwy on the seaward side. Acting as a barrier to communication, they also make a defensive shield behind which the men of Ardudwy retired after eastwards raids. The hills are still a formidable barrier, stretching for 13 miles from the Vale of Ffestiniog in the north to the Mawddach estuary in the south, uncrossed throughout by any road. The Roman Steps, a beautifully paved section of what is probably a packhorse way, crosses the hills north of Rhinog Fawr, while between the summits of Rhinog Fach and Rhinog Fawr is another ancient pass at Bwlch Drws-Ardudwy. Here on a day of mist and drizzling rain we came upon a herd of nine wild goats browsing peacefully at the head of the pass. Very possibly these and two other small herds in this area are the last wild goats in Wales.

On the western approach to Bwlch Drws-Ardudwy, at the head of Cwm Nantcol, is the ancient farm of Maes-y-garnedd which has a surprising link with a major upheaval in history. Here in this remote spot was born Colonel

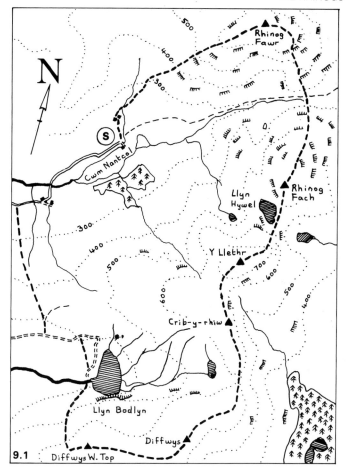

9.1

John Jones who married Catherine the sister of Oliver Cromwell. He entered history by putting his name to the death warrant of Charles I in 1649, but met his end at the Restoration in 1660 when he was hung, drawn and quartered.

Although in common with many other mountains there is no right of way along the ridge, stiles have been erected and most of the area is now covered by Tir Cymen (see page 133).

ROUTE DESCRIPTION

RHINOG FAWR *(Big Threshold)*

From the parking place at the road end by the farm gate, two footpaths are signposted. One heads straight for Bwlch Drws-Ardudwy, the door of Ardudwy, while the other sets off northwards over the shoulder of Rhinog Fawr. There is only one easy way up Rhinog Fawr and this shoulder route is the key. On the other sides the mountain is defended by deep heather and rough rocks, of which enough will be met on the continuation to Rhinog Fach.

Walk north up the lane to the house, Nantcol, into the fields beyond and climb to cross a wall at an obvious ladder stile. There is no sign of the right of way marked on the map, so head north-east, climbing steadily over reedy ground, past a ruined barn, towards the dip in the skyline to the left of the rocky south-west ridge. From about the 400m contour there is a cairned path up the left flank of the ridge, well away from the rocks and this is by far the easiest way up Rhinog Fawr. Becoming steadily clearer, the path passes below some sheepfolds then climbs to reach a ladder stile at the highest point on the wall beside a faded sign proclaiming that this is a nature reserve. Just over a quarter of a mile further is the flat, stony summit with a large partially collapsed cairn, an OS trig point and a windshelter. It is a magnificent viewpoint from which to admire the mountains of Snowdonia.

RHINOG FACH *(Little Threshold)*

The descent initially is eastwards where an encouragingly clear path from a cairn raises hopes of an easy descent. Soon however the path plays hide and seek among the rocks. We have never managed to follow the same route twice, but sooner or later and heading generally south, Bwlch Drws-Ardudwy is reached.

The ascent of Rhinog Fach, although over 1000ft of rough climb, has a path all the way. There is a feeling of great spaciousness about the top with long views towards Rhinog Fawr and also both seawards and over the forests to the east. A cairn at the southern end marks the highest point where a wall comes up from the east to finish beside it.

Y LLETHR *(The Slope)*

Fortunately there is much less descent to the next col. Follow the wall down eastwards and then south on a steep path which descends to the bwlch where steep, smooth slabs plunge into Llyn Hywel to the right while further down on the left is Llyn y Bi, magpie lake.

A clear path follows the wall and, trending away from it, climbs the steep slopes of Y Llethr. As the angle eases, the wall is re-joined. Turn right and the summit, a large cairn on the flat and featureless grassy top is soon reached.

CRIB-Y-RHIW *(Ridge of the Hill)*

The walking is now mainly on grass and a considerable contrast to the earlier

Hafod-y-Brenhin below Y Llethr

painfully slow progress. The navigation is also very easy as there is a wall to follow all the way. In fact if it is misty you could easily pass over this next top without noticing it, which is what we did and so had to go all the way back another day to be able to report that there is no cairn, nor any other distinguishing mark on this minor top! The highest point is a grass and heather knoll to the right of the wall at the far end of the ridge. In clear weather there are good views ahead to the dipping rock strata, an eroded syncline, of Diffwys and of the waterfall into Llyn Bodlyn.

DIFFWYS *(Precipice)*
Continuing along the wall, the path briefly parts company to avoid the ascent of a minor bump on the ridge, and then rejoins it to climb to the top of Diffwys. A ladder stile enables the OS trig point to be reached, which has views of the Mawddach estuary ahead, while behind the Rhinog range stretches away to the north. On the eastern slopes are the remains of a manganese mine.

DIFFWYS WEST TOP
Descending westwards by the wall it is difficult at first to believe that the next rise on the ridge is higher than the tops to the south-west as they appear to overtop it significantly. Soon however the deception is realised and heights regain their proper perspective, but the top is unmarked and a mere bump on

the ridge, so hurry on with the descent towards Llyn Bodlyn, which although a reservoir created for Barmouth in 1890, fits naturally into the scene with fine cliffs above a wild cwm. The rare deep-water fish the char can be found here. A line north-west at first is advisable to ensure that the descent stays on the grassy slopes avoiding the cliffs.

At one time the main route from Harlech to Dolgellau crossed this cwm at the old bridge, still shown as Pont-Scethin, but it is not necessary to go down as far to cross the stream as there is a bridge at the outflow of the reservoir. The reservoir track should then be followed for a short way before short-cutting across the moor to regain the track lower down. The ridge on the right now must be crossed. A path starts off towards the bwlch, but then turns up the ridge towards Y Llethr, so leave it to cross a ladder stile at the bwlch where a path re-emerges to lead gently downhill towards Cwm Nantcol. The public right of way is shown on the OS map as rather improbably crossing some way to the left and much higher up the slope. This looks like a mapper's error especially as there is a marker stone on the natural route. An easy descent with fine views of both the Rhinogs and Y Llethr soon brings you to the road. Turn right for the last unfenced mile back to the starting point.

WALK 9.2 THE NORTHERN RHINOGS

SUMMITS:	Moel Ysgyfarnogod	2044ft (623m)
	Foel Penolau	2014ft (614m)
DISTANCE:	6 miles	
ASCENT:	1250 feet	
MAPS:	OS Landranger sheet 124	
	Explorer OL18 - Harlech, Porthmadog & Bala / Y Bala	
STARTING POINT:	(124-629342) The end of the minor road which runs east from Glan-y-wern, 3 miles north of Harlech. A few cars may be parked on the verge.	

These two summits at the northern end of the Rhinogs are separated from Rhinog Fawr three miles to the south by some of the wildest, roughest and most attractive wilderness in Wales. The rock scenery is a maze of short steep walls, extensive smooth slabs and everywhere lies the scattered debris of ancient glaciers. As the rock walls are set mainly at right angles to the ridge the resulting succession of alternating ascents and descents reduces progress to a crawl, but although walking along the ridge is slow it is never boring as the rocks present a continuous series of fresh problems to be solved.

There is however an easy and very pleasant approach to these summits

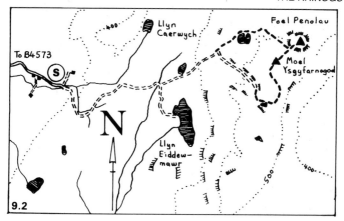

which, while avoiding most of the difficulties, nevertheless is a good introduction to this lovely area. The route follows an old mine track into the hills to pass between the twin lakes of Llyn Eiddew-bach and Llyn Eiddew-mawr, the ivy lakes, providing the easiest walking in the whole of the northern Rhinogs and and enjoyable half day.

After having been introduced to this western approach while staying at Plas Tan-y-bwlch, the Snowdonia National Park Study Centre, we subsequently explored the opposite flanks of these hills. But in comparison the eastern side is dreary and rather too close to Trawsfynydd Power Station.

The rocks of the Rhinog range, which date from the Cambrian age, contain large amounts of low-grade manganese ore which was mined hereabouts on a small scale. These miners must have been the tidiest that ever existed as the old mines are at first glance next to invisible. The spoil has been banked up neatly to either side and there are none of the untidy and desolate waste tips produced elsewhere by both slate quarries and copper mines.

ROUTE DESCRIPTION

MOEL YSGYFARNOGOD *(Bare Hill of the Hare)*
Go right at the road end over the Afon Eisingrug and follow the gated old mine track for just over a mile and a half, passing between Llyn Eiddew-bach and Llyn Eiddew-mawr. Continuing uphill, on the right a collection of boulders lies abandoned by the ice on the bedrock. The track turns right on a banked up section to wind round halfway up the cliffs past the separate bays of the old manganese mines and at its end a rocky defile leads through the cliffs to arrive

On the Rhinogs, the northern end

at the tiny triangular lake of Llyn Du, black lake. The track continues north a little further, passing more workings and a shelter, with an extensive panorama of the eastern slopes now in view. But all good things must come to an end and the track abruptly terminates with the twin objectives of the walk very conveniently just ahead. A faint path skirts round to the left of the rocks to vanish beyond. Climb north up the re-entrant to the left of the main summit of Moel Ysgyfarnogod to avoid the cliffs, and join the ridge. A short stroll right leads to the grassy top which has an OS trig point and a roughly constructed windshelter. To the south lie Rhinog Fawr, Rhinog Fach and Cadair Idris, with to the east the Arenigs, Arans and Berwyns and to the north the mountains of northern Snowdonia.

FOEL PENOLAU *(Top of the Light Bare Hill)*
Head north-east directly for the summit, which is only quarter of a mile away, aiming for a gully up which you can scramble. This is a fascinating mountain. Surrounded by vertical cliffs, Foel Penolau is one of the best defended

mountain tops in Wales. On reaching the top of the gully, at first sight the glacier-planed slabs, which have been split to form vertical fissures, remind one strongly of the limestone pavements in Yorkshire, although this is not limestone, but rock of volcanic origin. The scrambling is not quite over as further rock walls, about 10ft high, defend two separated platforms of rock each with a cairn. As they are given exactly the same height by the OS, it will be necessary to scramble to the top of both!

For the easiest descent return via the same gully and then head north-west across the moor to a sheepfold and join a track which leads from more old mine workings to Llyn Dywarchen, turf lake. Pass the lake to the north and then follow the old mine road all the way back to the starting point.

WALK 9.3 Y GARN

SUMMITS:	Y Garn	2064ft (629m)
DISTANCE:	5 miles	
ASCENT:	2000 feet	
MAPS:	OS Landranger sheet 124	
	Explorer OL18 - Harlech, Porthmadog & Bala / Y Bala	
STARTING POINT:	(124-727243) Ganllwyd, 4 miles north of Dolgellau on the A470. National Trust car park, toilets.	

Y Garn, on the edge of the Coed-y-Brenin forest to the north of Dolgellau, is separated from the main ridge of the Rhinogs three miles to the west by rough moorland and the wooded valley of the Afon Cwm-mynach. Although there are rocky areas on its slopes the character of the mountain is essentially that of the southern grassy Rhinogs.

For us it was fourth time lucky. Our first visit to Y Garn was in diabolical weather. The forecasters had promised a fine weekend so, laden with backpacking gear plus a reluctant son, we struggled to the top. The wind was so strong we had to crawl to gain the summit cairn and the rain was coming down in bucketfuls. Clad expensively in Gore-tex from head to toe we were nevertheless soaked to the skin. On our second visit it wasn't actually raining all the time and we explored the southern slopes, but we were very little wiser afterwards as you could hardly see your hand before you, never mind the shape of the mountain. We were really looking forward to a third visit, but it was only on our fourth ascent that we were finally rewarded by the extensive panorama from the top.

The eastern slopes of Y Garn boast an old gold mine, less well known than the one at Bontddu from which traditionally the wedding rings of the royal family are made. Around 1840 gold was discovered in the lead mines of Berthlwyd and in 1862 a company was formed which installed the latest machinery. By the 1890s more than 30 men were employed in the New California mine, but alas it proved unprofitable and the mine was eventually closed in 1914. The gold is found in seams of quartz which explains the white spoil. Ruins of a few buildings, open levels and white quartz tips are now all that remain.

The spectacular waterfall of the Afon Gamlan, Rhaiadr Du, the black falls, is 65ft high, and is so called because the water cascades over black rocks. William Maddocks (of Porthmadog fame) built a footpath to the falls and they were visited by the famous painters of the day. The falls are in the midst of oak woodland which now belongs to the National Trust. Oak bark from here was once shipped to Ireland and Scotland to be used in the tanning of leather.

Coed-y-Brenin is a working forest and about 41,000 tons of timber are produced annually. Logs are used in the building industry and pulp wood is sent to the new paper mill at Shotton in Clwyd. The nearby Maesgwm Visitor Centre is well worth a visit. There are many interesting displays plus a café and information centre. It has the added attraction of being free, and is a very suitable place in which to pass the time while you wonder if it ever stops raining in this part of North Wales!

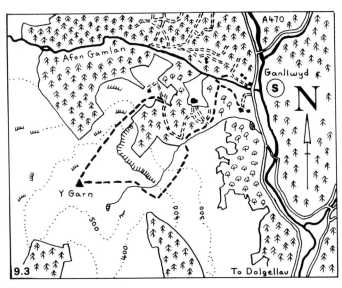

ROUTE DESCRIPTION

Y GARN *(The Cairn)*

Take the metalled road beside the chapel at the bridge and at the first bend turn left on the National Trust waymarked path to the falls. Crossing the footbridge below the Rhaiadr Du continue left through the wood along the main path. At a signpost to Cefn Coch mines turn right and follow the waymarked main path in the wood. Emerging from the oak woodland to cross the Nant Las, blue green stream, turn right through the field to join a road which then crosses a bridge back into the forest. At the first junction in about 100 yards, turn left then almost immediately left again on a track which runs parallel to the edge of the forest. On meeting a forest road which hairpins down on the right, go left through a gate onto the open hillside. Crossing the stream for a third time to the deserted mine buildings, climb up the ridge to the south-west on easy grassy slopes passing the old gold mine workings.

At the top a stout wall separates the National Trust land from the hillside beyond. These sturdy walls on Y Garn are devoid of any gates, but now there is a stile, so leave the National Trust land and head west for the summit which is less than half a mile away past a large sheepfold. A cairn stands on top of a rocky knoll on the grassy summit. The wide panorama stretches from Cadair Idris, past the Mawddach estuary to take in the whole of the Rhinog range and Llyn Trawsfynydd with the high mountains of Snowdonia beyond, while to the east lie the Arenigs and the Arans.

For the return head north-east and re-cross the same wall further along, then follow the next wall down north-east on its left-hand side over Ffrîdd Gwndwn-uchaf. Where a cross wall is met, go through a narrow gateway and descend rightwards to a field gate by the corner of the forest. Follow the edge of the forest down to join the forest road. Turn right and walk downhill to the hairpin bend where the outward route is taken back as far as the signpost. Turn right here to the Plas Dolymelynllyn Hotel and then left down the hotel drive to the main road.

Cadair Idris from Cyfrwy

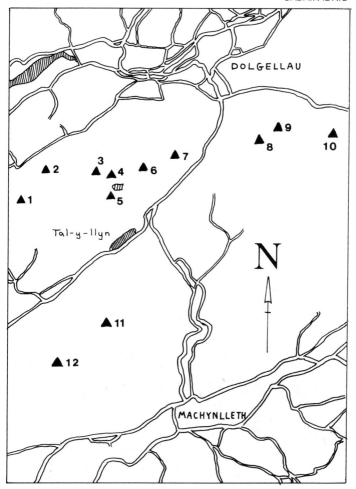

10. CADAIR IDRIS

CHAPTER 10: CADAIR IDRIS

TOP	NAME	HEIGHT	GRID REF	WALK No.
1	Craig-y-llyn	622m	124-666120 SH	10.2
2	Tyrrau Mawr	661m	124-677135 SH	10.2
3	Cyfrwy	811m	124-704134 SH	10.1
4	Cadair Idris	893m	124-711130 SH	10.1
5	Craig Cwm Amarch	791m	124-711121 SH	10.1
6	Mynydd Moel	863m	124-728137 SH	10.1
7	Gau Graig	683m	124-744141 SH	10.1
8	Waun-oer	670m	124-786148 SH	10.3
9	Cribin Fawr	659m	124-795153 SH	10.3
10	Maesglase	676m	124-817150 SH	10.3
11	Tarren y Gesail	667m	124-711059 SH	10.4
12	Tarrenhendre	634m	135-683042 SH	10.4

Llyn Cau

WALK 10.1 CADAIR IDRIS

SUMMITS:	Craig Cwm Amarch	2595ft (791m)
	Cyfrwy	2661ft (811m)
	Cadair Idris	2930ft (893m)
	Mynydd Moel	2831ft (863m)
	Gau Graig	2241ft (683m)

DISTANCE: 10½ miles

ASCENT: 3400 feet

MAPS: OS Landranger sheet 124
Explorer OL23 - Cadair Idris & Llyn Tegid

STARTING
POINT: (124-732115) Minffordd, one mile north-east of Tal-y-llyn. Car park and toilets.

Cadair Idris, the Chair of Idris, only a stone's throw from the sea for the giant after whom it is named, is truly a whole group of mountains, perhaps one Munro in Scottish terms although it fails to qualify as such by a mere 70ft. The highest top is Penygadair, but this has assumed the title of Cadair Idris by popular assent and of the southernmost hills of Snowdonia it is by far the most frequented. The nearness to the sea seems to produce some wild weather with the mountain providing the first major obstacle to the westerly winds.

The chair of Idris (who may well have been a seventh-century Welsh hero rather than a mythical giant) is the north-facing cwm containing Llyn y Gadair; the spelling G rather than C is correct, an instance of what is called mutation and one of the most difficult things in the Welsh language to master. The even finer east-facing cwm in which Llyn Cau, shut-in lake, is cradled is the heart of the Cadair Idris National Nature Reserve where, despite the sheep, the base-rich rocks support plants which are only found in similarly favoured small pockets elsewhere in Snowdonia.

Kilvert records in his famous diary his ascent on 13 June 1871 of 'the stoniest, dreariest, most desolate mountain I was ever on'. As it was raining steadily and he could see little but the mist, one can sympathise with him. His guide told him about the Ordnance Survey visit, '"The Captain of the surveying company had his tent pitched on the top of Cader Idris for 3 summer months and never left the place. He had 18 men to wait upon him. And how many clear views do you think he got in that time?" "Twelve", I hazarded. "Nine", he said.' They then entered the 'rude 2-roomed hut', which the guide said had been built by his father and here Kilvert ate his lunch of bread and butter and hard-boiled egg. This solidly built hut still stands by the cairn providing welcome shelter on similar days, but guides at 5 shillings are no longer available!

The northern cliffs stretch in an almost unbroken line for over four miles from Cyfrwy in the west to Gau Graig in the east and ascent by Llwybr Cadno, Fox's Path, the only weakness, is actively discouraged due to erosion. As however the Minffordd path is an excellent approach, there is no problem and the cliffs can be appreciated as one follows the top edge out to Gau Graig.

As well as the plants, the geology of Cadair Idris is particularly interesting, the mountain itself being composed of the hard crystalline rocks of granophyre. It is said to be an excellent example of the formation of rock strata during the Ordovician Period and the later erosion of these rocks by glaciers formed the impressive cwms. Tal-y-llyn Lake, or Llyn Mwyngil, is towards the end of the 12-mile long geological Bala fault which runs south from Bala Lake to Cadair Idris.

ROUTE DESCRIPTION

CRAIG CWM AMARCH *(Amarch Valley Rock)*
Go through the gate beside the toilet block and follow the path which leads through an avenue of trees across the river, then bends left over a bridge to another gate and the entrance to the nature reserve. The path climbs steeply to the left of Nant Cadair through the wood beside the falls and after leaving the trees, flattens out and passes a trial enclosure. This on our last visit was a mass of golden yellow bog asphodel, elsewhere totally absent due to the sheep. Shortly the path forks, the right-hand branch continuing towards Llyn Cau. This is worth a detour, an attractive lake enclosed on three sides by cliffs. There is a weakness in the cliffs to the west of Llyn Cau by which Cadair Idris may be approached more directly, but as the first objective would thus be bypassed, return from the lake and take the left fork which climbs steeply to gain the top of the cliffs on the south side of Llyn Cau. An undulating section, with breathtaking views down the gullies to the lake, is followed by a short steeper ascent to the top where there is a fence crossed by a ladder stile. The summit is the rocks immediately on the right over the stile.

CYFRWY *(The Saddle)*
Follow the ridge north with the precipice of Craig Cau to the right and descend to a col. Cyfrwy is an out and back detour, but although the map suggests contouring round to avoid unnecessary ascent, the intervening ground is very rough and the navigation difficult in mist, it is easier to gain height using the clear path heading for Cadair Idris. When the path turns north-east and then flattens out before the final steep pull up to the summit of Cadair Idris, turn off left through the rocks to gain the Pony Path coming up from the west.

Turn left and follow this cairned path gently down until it turns left, then using the cliff edge and the occasional cairn as a guide head north-west to the summit of Cyfrwy which has a small cairn and a windshelter perched on the edge of the cliffs.

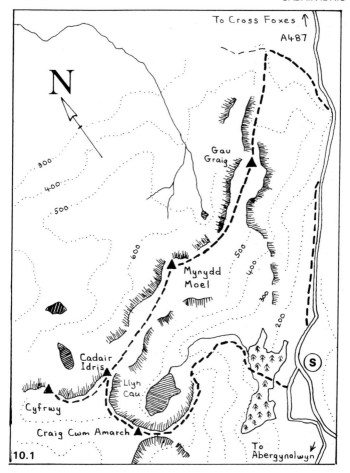

To Cross Foxes ↑
A487

N

Gau
Graig

300
400
500
600

500

400

Mynydd
Moel

300

200

Cadair
Idris

Llyn
Cau

Cyfrwy

Craig Cwm Amarch

S

To
Abergynolwyn ↓

10.1

CADAIR IDRIS *(Idris' Chair)*

Returning to join the Pony Path, this leads to the summit of Cadair Idris and
its white painted OS trig point reached by a few steps. The view stretches from
Pumlumon in the south to Snowdon in the north and on a clear day it is
possible to see Ireland. The roomy refuge, which has been re-roofed, may be
cursed as an unwelcome intrusion in the hills or gratefully entered in order to

Craig Cwm Amarch

eat one's sandwiches. The weather has a considerable influence on one's feelings on this point. On a wet July day we met and chatted there with the only people we had seen all day, a man in a smart black kilt and a lady who kindly corrected our Welsh pronunciation. The black kilt, it transpired, was not the garb of a Scotsman, but an ingenious solution to the problem of wet shorts, a dustbin liner wrapped around to protect the shorts when wearing a waterproof top!

MYNYDD MOEL *(Bare Mountain)*
The path east to Mynydd Moel follows the edge of the cliffs which present an almost impregnable barrier to approaches to Cadair Idris from the north. A

Tal-y-llyn

mile of easy going with superb downward views brings you to a ladder stile and the summit of Mynydd Moel is then about 100 yards beyond. There is a large cairn and a twin compartment windshelter on the stony summit.

GAU GRAIG *(Hollow Rock)*

Descend east with the ground gradually steepening on a good cairned path. At the foot of the steep section there is a useful spring and from here there is a fence to follow along the ridge which can be rather boggy in places. About two-thirds of a mile after the spring there are two stiles where a fence comes in from the right. Cross these and head up to the summit, which has a rough cairn enigmatically set in the centre of a walled enclosure.

Descend north to cross the fence and follow a good path down the north-east ridge crossing two ladder stiles over joining walls. At a third stile, cross over this to the right-hand side of the wall, continue to follow it for a short way and then veer away right over pathless terrain to join the right of way, an old road, which heads south-east towards the A487. A waymark and a stile at the stream crossing by some sheepfolds assists route-finding and the path emerges onto the road at a stile.

Turn right on the main road where motorists race each other over the pass and there is very little verge in places. However in half a mile the busy road can be left in favour of the disused old road on the right which runs through Cwm Rhwyddfor, parallel to the road down to Minffordd, where for a final short section the main road is rejoined back to the start.

WALK 10.2 WEST OF CADAIR IDRIS

SUMMITS:	Tyrrau Mawr	2169ft (661m)
	Craig-y-llyn	2041ft (622m)
DISTANCE:	10 miles	
ASCENT:	2640 feet	
MAPS:	OS Landranger sheet 124	
	Explorer OL23 - Cadair Idris & Llyn Tegid	

STARTING
POINT: (124-672088) Car park opposite the chapel in the hamlet of Llanfihangel-y-pennant, one mile due north of Abergynolwyn. Toilets.

A pony track runs from the tiny hamlet of Llanfihangel-y-pennant northwards over the hills towards Llyn Gwernan and Dolgellau. Walkers reaching the top of the pass turn eastwards towards Cadair Idris and few indeed are the feet heading the other way. These grassy and heather-covered hills west of Cadair Idris are much lower and can provide a pleasant alternative for a lazy summer day or when the higher summits are hidden in the clouds. After one scorching day here, with heat haze obscuring the distant views, we descended to swim in the refreshingly cool Tal-y-llyn Lake. On a return visit in February the rain wet us just as thoroughly, but wet or dry you will meet very few people on these hills.

The Pennant valley is famous for Bird Rock, the ruined Castell y Bere and for Mary Jones. It was from here in 1800 that Mary Jones aged 16, set out to walk about 25 miles to Bala to buy a Welsh bible from the Reverend Thomas Charles. Mary had saved up her money and completed the long journey in bare feet, to spare her shoes. The last copy had been sold and no more were to be printed, but the pastor was so impressed by her efforts that he gave her his own bible. From the inspiration of this event grew the British and Foreign Bible Society. A monument to Mary has been erected in the ruins of Tyn-y-ddol, the cottage in which she lived.

Castell y Bere is a surprisingly large stone fortification. It must have been very impressive in its day for it was one of the biggest castles built by the Welsh. It is worth exploring at the end of the walk; the ruins are well preserved and open at all times. The castle was begun in 1221 by Llewelyn ap Iorwerth, Prince of North Wales, who needed a fortification in this area. His grandson Llewelyn ap Gruffydd became Prince of all Wales and strengthened it. When he died in 1282, his brother Dafydd held it until it was besieged by 3000 men and fell to Edward I. Last of all the Welsh castles to fall, Castell y Bere was then occupied by the English. There was an unsuccessful rebellion in 1294, and after this the castle became ruined.

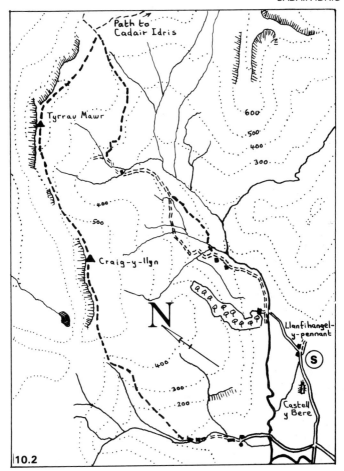

10.2

Craig yr Aderyn, bird rock, dominates the Dysynni valley. It is a nesting site for cormorants with 25 to 30 pairs breeding every year. It is about five miles from the sea and is the only inland nesting site for these birds in Europe. The sea once came up to the foot of the cliff and although the sea level has dropped about 60ft over the centuries, the birds still return. On the summit at a height of 760ft are the remains of an Iron Age hill fort.

ROUTE DESCRIPTION

TYRRAU MAWR *(Large Towers)*

From the chapel at Llanfihangel-y-pennant walk up the lane to the Tyn-y-ddol monument, crossing over the Afon Cadair, chair river, by a new bridge next to the old one. Turn right through a gate and follow the left bank of the river upstream to Gwastadfryn, where the road becomes a bridleway. The track now climbs uphill quite steeply. By a ruined barn leave the main track, the next section of which is private, to follow a waymarked path which crosses a small stream by an old slate footbridge. The bridleway zigzags uphill and then levels out to rejoin the main track. Follow the bridleway signs uphill to Hafotty Gwastadfryn, where there are sheep pens. Fork right and follow the waymarks to zigzag uphill on a grassy track on the bridleway high above the stream and round to the col.

At this point the old Pony Path to Cadair Idris comes up from the other side of the ridge and continues east to the summit. Our route however goes west following the fence along the ridge over a rocky summit, Carnedd Llwyd, grey cairn, which is marked with ancient cairns, to the less interesting but higher summit of Tyrrau Mawr. There is no cairn, just a smooth grassy top above a steep drop by a ladder stile. There are extensive views of the Mawddach estuary and Barmouth Bay, while to the south you can look back towards Llanfihangel-y-pennant. The ridge ahead is most impressive with a precipitous drop to the west.

CRAIG-Y-LLYN *(Rock of the Lake)*

Follow the ridge south-west for about a mile along the fence, first down to the col, where it passes near to a new bulldozed track on the left, and then steeply up over grass to the summit. The highest point is marked by a few slates and two white quartz stones. There is an old roll of fence wire which from a distance so resembles a trig point that if it were covered with snow it could well be mistaken for one. To the west lies the expanse of Barmouth Bay and below Llynau Gregennen.

To descend, continue south-west down the ridge beside the fence to an excavated ancient cairn, then by the unfenced edge to a field corner at the col where you follow the fence down left to a new bulldozed road. Walk left along the road to a junction and then head downhill south-west to pick up the right of way at a small gate by some sheepfolds. This leads down to a ladder stile and then crosses the field to Nant-Caw-fawr Farm. Continue along the farm track to Bodilan Fach where a stile to the left of the chapel leads through the fields beside the river to a bridge at Maes-y-llan, then back along a lane to Llanfihangel-y-pennant.

WALK 10.3 WEST OF DINAS MAWDDWY

SUMMITS:	Waun-oer	2198ft (670m)
	Cribin Fawr	2162ft (659m)
	Maesglase	2218ft (676m)
DISTANCE:	12 miles	
ASCENT:	3300 feet	
MAPS:	OS Landranger sheet 124	
	Explorer OL23 - Cadair Idris & Llyn Tegid	
STARTING POINT:	(124-778102) Aberllefenni, 6 miles north of Machynlleth. Car parking by the side of the road.	

These three summits are situated to the south of the A470 Cross Foxes to Dinas Mawddwy road. It is a pleasant and little-known ridge walk with the ground dropping steeply over rough crags to the north while the southern slopes are covered by the vast Dyfi Forest.

The walk starts from Aberllefenni, a village situated deep in the forest in the heart of the old slate mining area. A slate specialist's workshop reminds one of this valley's industrial past and there is also a Field Studies Centre, a Forestry Commission picnic area and a forest trail. Although not obvious from the map, it is possible to drive through the forest on a very scenic road all the

Cottages in Cwm Ratgoed

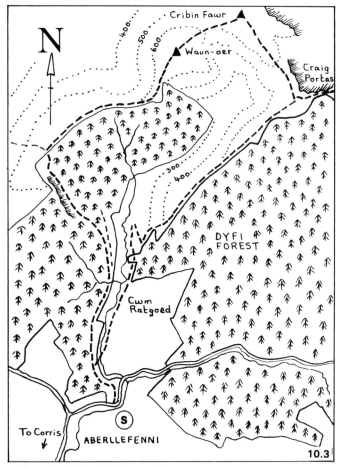

way from Aberllefenni to Aberangell.

    As with many ridge walks the problem is how to return to the starting point. For those with two cars, or a non-walking companion, the ridge may be gained by a right of way a couple of miles south of Cross Foxes and can then be followed all the way to Dinas Mawddwy passing the dramatic waterfall at Craig Maesglase. Alternatively you can descend through the forest to Aberangell. The solution adopted here is to make a horseshoe above Cwm

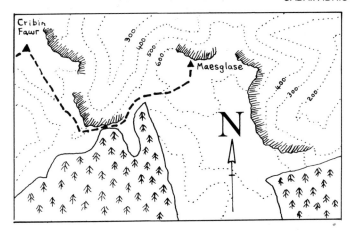

Ratgoed. Although an out and back journey must be made from Craig Portas to Maesglase, this is no great hardship as the return only takes half an hour and the scenery is well worth a second look.

ROUTE DESCRIPTION

WAUN-OER *(Cold Moor)*

By the Field Studies Centre take the track which leads up Cwm Ratgoed. At the bridge, in about half a mile, cross over Nant Ceiswyn and walk up a broad track by the side of the little stream. The whole valley is very quiet with ruins of old quarries and fences made of slate. At Ffynnon-Badarn, the waymarked path leads over a footbridge and round this pretty little cottage to climb up an unexpected new flight of steps to a forest road. The right of way shown on the OS map has been diverted so carry on up the road for another quarter of a mile, past a waterfall, to where a waymarked footpath slants up through the woods. From here it is a steady pull up through the forest to the summit ridge, first on an easy grassy footpath then, after crossing another road, on a wide rough ride. The path climbs high above the meandering river with the line of the ridge stretching impressively round the head of the cwm.

On gaining the ridge, Cadair Idris and the Rhinogs are seen ahead. The walking and route-finding is now easy, just turn right at the fence and follow it! Waun-oer is reached after an undulating mile and a half. The grassy summit is marked by a very smart round stone trig point on a little outcrop of rock, while on an adjacent knoll is a small radio mast.

CRIBIN FAWR *(Big Serrated Ridge)*

Staying by the fence, the ridge dips steeply almost to a forest road and then a sharp climb up onto Cribin Fawr leads to a stile on the summit. Cross left over the fence which you have been following and hunt around for the highest point a little beyond the stile. The top is flat tussocky grass with one or two bits looking higher than the rest. When you have finally decided which tussock is the highest, admire the view which is quite extensive with the Rhinogs to the north-west and the Arans to the north-east while beyond are the higher mountains of Snowdonia.

MAESGLASE *(Blue Meadow)*

Head back to the stile and follow the fence south-east to pick up a faint path, with good views of the Tarren Hills to the right. At the col cross to the other side of the fence to climb Craig Portas, keeping left near the awesome drop in order to bypass the summit. Rejoining the fence beyond Craig Portas, switchback over to Maesglase past steep gullies which cut almost into the path. At a ladder stile follow the fence up to the left, then head over the tussocky moor to the cairn on Craig Rhiw-erch. In 1996 Professor Tim Jones wrote to say he thought this top looked higher than the traditional summit. "So what," we thought, "they often do". But spurred into action for the Second

Icicles on Maesglase

Edition, we surveyed it on a glorious sunny afternoon and discovered he was right. Craig Rhiw-erch is indeed about 2m higher than Maen Du, making a new highest point in the Dovey Hills.

Retrace your steps for one and a half miles back to Craig Portas and then follow the old boundary fence south-west over Mynydd Dolgoed with the occasional stone marked EB. Below on the left are the vast expanses of the Dyfi Forest; a complete blanket of green apart from one or two tiny fields which have been spared.

At the end of the ridge the ground drops steeply through scrubby woodland. About halfway down the slope a stile on the left enters the forest by a warning notice about chasms in the ground. Turn right here and go down the old right of way, now almost disappeared, to a gate by a ruined barn. Crossing the field, turn left on the old track which passes Ratgoed Hall, not yet ruined, and some derelict quarry buildings. Above on the left are old mines, tunnels and levels. Soon the cottage of Ffynnon-Badarn, on the other side of the river, is passed and the outward route is followed back to Aberllefenni.

WALK 10.4 THE TARREN HILLS

SUMMITS:	Tarrenhendre	2080ft (634m)
	Tarren y Gesail	2188ft (667m)
DISTANCE:	9 miles	
ASCENT:	2900 feet	
MAPS:	OS Landranger sheet 124 & 135	
	Explorer OL23 - Cadair Idris & Llyn Tegid	
STARTING POINT:	(124-678069) Abergynolwyn village, on the B4405, 7 miles north-east of Tywyn. Car park, toilets.	

The Tarren hills above the little village of Abergynolwyn are unfrequented, often quite deserted. This is a good place to go on a busy Bank Holiday if you want to be alone, though Abergynolwyn is popular enough in summer as it is the terminus of the Talyllyn railway. The hills are grassy with forests on their flanks and open moorland higher up.

Abergynolwyn was once an important centre of the slate industry. Before 1860 it was made up of two tiny hamlets, with 15 cottages, inn, chapel, mill and a small tannery. In 1864 Bryn-Eglwys Quarry was bought by William Maconnell who mechanised it, built houses for his workers in the village and constructed the Talyllyn railway. There were also barracks for the men in the quarry itself, but after less than a century of industrial activity it closed in 1948.

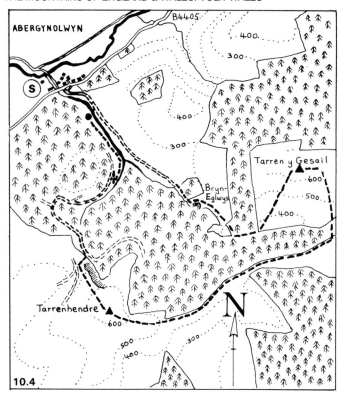

10.4

The 7-mile long railway was built in 1866 to transport the slate from the quarry to Tywyn, and to provide a passenger service. It is a narrow-gauge line with a width of 2ft 3in. It was initially preserved by the last quarry owner and then by the Talyllyn Railway Preservation Society which was formed in 1951. The mineral railway, which runs from Abergynolwyn to Nant Gwernol, was restored by the society and the line was opened for passengers in 1976. Trains run from April to October. The new footbridge over Nant Gwernol, at the station, was formally opened by the chairman of the Wales Tourist Board in 1980.

This part of the Dyfi Forest was bought by the Forestry Commission after the Bryn-Eglwys Quarry closed. The timber is used for chipboard, pit props, fencing and paper pulp. Recreation in the forest is increasing and woodland walks are waymarked from the station.

ROUTE DESCRIPTION

TARRENHENDRE *(Knoll of the Winter Dwelling)*

Go up the very steep minor road opposite the Railway Inn in the centre of Abergynolwyn and turn right on a good footpath signposted to Nant Gwernol Station. The path through attractive woodland follows the left bank of the river above deep green pools until, at the footbridge, it crosses the stream to the station.

A signpost points the way up the steps to a path which zigzags up the hill, following yellow markers, to the old winding house at the top of the Allt Willt incline. The incline and the winding house with its massive drum are being restored by members of the railway society.

Follow the line of the old railway high above the river until the gorge of the Nant Moelfre is reached with the remains of an old incline on the far side. Turn right and follow the Nant Moelfre upstream along a path which is waymarked with blue markers. After a sharp right bend, it continues climbing to join a main forest road. Turn left and tramp uphill on the forest roads. Ignore the first left fork and shortly pass an old ruin on the left. You are now, quite correctly, heading directly away from Tarrenhendre, but forest paths seldom go in the direction you want. The track levels out in quarter of a mile and you turn left to pass a small pond on the left. Continue round left and you are now heading towards the hills again.

A path on the far edge of the evergreens, which have filled up a gap in the larches, leads to the cliffs of Tarrenhendre. Scramble up a steep shaley slope to reach a gully to the right of the cliffs. The fence at the top leads directly to the summit and the going will be found easier on the far side. As the highest point is reached re-cross the fence by a stile to the summit which is a peat hag crowned by a small cairn near the junction of two fences. Another fence beyond crosses the site of an ancient cairn.

TARREN Y GESAIL *(Knoll of the Hollow)*

Follow the fence east downhill to Foel y Geifr, bare hill of the goats, along a broad grassy ridge with trees on the left and a steep drop on the right. There are good views of the Afon Dyfi to the right and of Cadair Idris to the left.

At the lowest point the corner of a mature forest is passed and then the path heads uphill to cross over a stile and along a little ridge through the trees. The path becomes indistinct and then, joining a better path beside a fence with a deep valley to the left, climbs steadily to a stile in the fence at the col.

Turn left to follow the fence which heads north-west steeply uphill over grass to join another fence on the ridge, by a cairn. This is not the summit. Turn left, heading west and walk over tussocky grass and heather to the summit which is marked by a stone OS trig point and small stone windshelter, although the OS give a spot height a metre higher about 50 yards east of the trig point, just to the right of the fence.

The return route lies through the disused Bryn-Eglwys, church hill, Quarry in the valley below. Descend gently over grass heading south-west to a track at the corner of the forest. Pass through a gate to follow the track by an empty reservoir with a tower sticking up forlornly and the lovely Pont Llaeron now leading to nowhere. This bridge is on the line of Llwybr Cadfan, Cadfan's Way, the old Pilgrims' Way from Machynlleth, by Bryn-Eglwys, to Abergynolwyn and Tywyn. It crossed the ridge at the lowest point and was reputed to lead to the holy island of Bardsey. Follow the track through the deserted quarries with an old winding house to the right and a magnificent waterfall to the left. Pass under the old incline at a collapsing bridge and through a new larch plantation. Footpath signs suddenly appear in the wilderness showing the way to join the tarmac road. This leads back to Abergynolwyn, passing close by the open chasm of the Bryn-Eglwys Quarry.

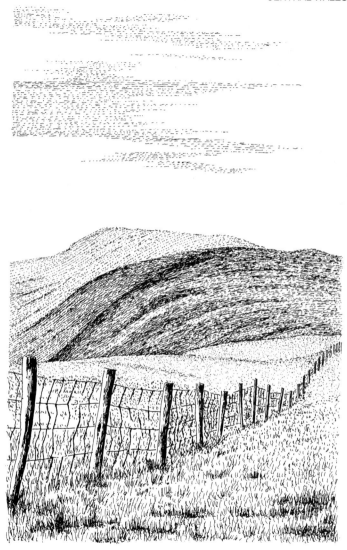

Pumlumon Fawr seen on the approach from Y Garn

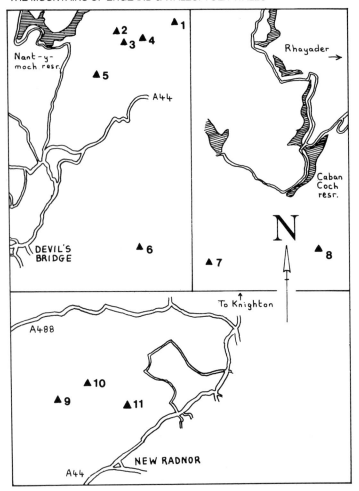

11. CENTRAL WALES

CHAPTER 11: CENTRAL WALES

TOP	NAME	HEIGHT	GRID REF	WALK No.
1	Pen Pumlumon Arwystli	741m	135-815878 SN	11.1
2	Pumlumon Fach	664m	135-787874 SN	11.1
3	Pumlumon Fawr	752m	135-790870 SN	11.1
4	Pen Pumlumon Llygad-bychan	727m	135-799871 SN	11.1
5	Y Garn	684m	135-776852 SN	11.1
6	Pen y Garn	610m	135-799771 SN	11.2
7	Drygarn Fawr	641m	147-862584 SN	11.3
8	Gorllwyn	613m	147-918591 SN	11.3
9	Great Rhos	660m	148-182639 SO	11.4
10	Black Mixen	650m	148-196644 SO	11.4
11	Bache Hill	610m	148-214636 SO	11.4

Drygarn Fawr

WALK 11.1 PUMLUMON

SUMMITS:	Y Garn	2244ft (684m)
	Pumlumon Fawr	2467ft (752m)
	Pumlumon Fach	2178ft (664m)
	Pen Pumlumon Llygad-bychan	2385ft (727m)
	Pen Pumlumon Arwystli	2431ft (741m)
NOTE:	The stream at Cwm Gwerin could be difficult to cross after heavy rain.	
DISTANCE:	11½ miles	
ASCENT:	2050 feet	
MAPS:	OS Landranger sheet 135, Explorer 213 & 214	
STARTING POINT:	(135-767869) The eastern side of the Nant-y-moch Reservoir, which is approached by minor roads from either Tal-y-bont or Ponterwyd. Ample parking on the verge.	

Pumlumon, hill of the five cairns, is the highest point in mid Wales. This grassy mountain range lies to the east of Aberystwyth, and uncrossed by roads forms a wilderness of some 80 square miles. The Forestry Commission with its regimented conifers are encroaching on the flanks of the hills and sheep farmers, seduced by EEC grants, have bulldozed rough roads across the wilderness, but still it is a little frequented area where we have walked all day without meeting anyone at all. The most frequented route to Pumlumon starts from the summit of the Eisteddfa Gurig Pass, but it is rather dreary and the return via the Hafren Forest and the dusty bulldozed roads passing the Nant Iago lead mine seems to go on for ever. To the north lies the wilderness and if you don't mind getting wet feet an exploration of this area adds another dimension to the walk. The mountain summits, crowned with Bronze Age burial mounds in a time when people had a proper respect for mountain tops, show that the area was not always so deserted. Abandoned mine workings too are reminders of more active times.

To the east of the range lies the Hafren Forest which takes its name from the Afon Hafren, River Severn. Tree planting began here in 1937 and now extends to over 15 square miles, the wood being used for the manufacture of paper pulp, chipboard and fencing material. Nant-y-moch in the centre of the area is a hydroelectric reservoir. Owain Glyndwr raised his standard here in 1401 and won a battle against Henry IV.

George Borrow wrote that Pumlumon though "it does not look much of a hill" was "famed because of three grand rivers of the world issue from its breast, the Hafren, the Rheidol and the Gwy." After climbing to the summit he visited the source of the Rheidol, which rising in Llyn Llygad Rheidol reaches

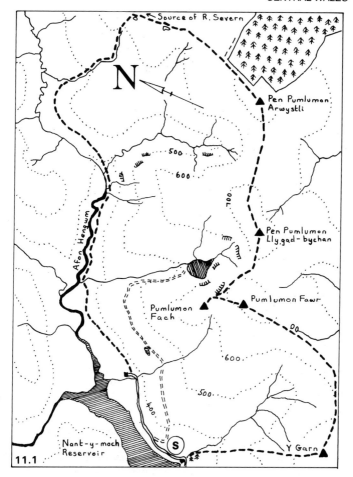

11.1

the sea in a speedy 16 miles. Next he went to the source of the Severn which flows for over 200 miles to the Bristol Channel. This rises in a swampy, peaty area above the Hafren Forest and the attractiveness of this spot varies considerably with the weather. After a long dry spell the spring shrinks to a murky evil-looking pond when it would surely be foolish to partake of the waters as Borrow did. After "taking possession of the Severn by drinking at its source" you would probably have to take possession of the nearest hospital! Borrow next nipped over to the source of the Wye in just 15 minutes and took possession of that as well.

ROUTE DESCRIPTION

Y GARN *(The Cairn)*

From the shores of the Nant-y-moch Reservoir it is an easy climb of just over 1000ft over grassy slopes to the summit of Y Garn. Cross the stile beside the Nant-y-moch, stream of the pigs, and climb up the north ridge. The summit is topped with an ancient cairn which has been refashioned to include a small windshelter. The Nant-y-moch Reservoir and dam can be seen below, while northwards the ridge leads to the main summit of Pumlumon Fawr with Pumlumon Fach to the left and Pen Pumlumon Llygad-bychan to the right.

PUMLUMON FAWR *(Big Five Stacks)*

In mist the forest fence is a good guide as it leads east for half a mile to the col and then heads north all the way to the summit of Pumlumon Fawr, which it crosses. In fine weather keep over to the top of the cwm for good views down into the Nant-y-moch valley and join the forest edge at a gate. The forest has sadly been nearly destroyed, the result of a fire in the mid 1980s. Continue

Pumlumon summit

by the fence for a couple of hundred yards, passing a fence post at the junction where a small label reminds you of Derek and Peter who erected it, then climb over to join the main path to Pumlumon Fawr. This passes two tiny lakes which disappear in dry weather and it is then an easy walk up to the flat grassy summit which has two large ancient cairns, three windshelters and an OS trig point. On a clear day distant views of Cadair Idris, the mountains of Snowdonia, the Brecon Beacons, the Malvern Hills and Cardigan Bay can be seen from here.

PUMLUMON FACH *(Little Five Stacks)*

A small cairn at the north end of the flat top of Pumlumon Fawr marks the descent to Pumlumon Fach down the north-west ridge. You can either skirt round or climb over the first top to the second which has a cairn on the top. The first top, although higher is only separated from Pumlumon Fawr by a rise of 42ft, however 64ft of ascent entitles the second to join the elite.

PEN PUMLUMON LLYGAD-BYCHAN *(Five Stacks Top of the Small Stream Source)*

Retrace your steps for a short way back up Pumlumon Fawr and then pick up a sheep trod which contours round above the cliffs that drop towards Llyn Llygad Rheidol. There are dramatic views of the cwm until the main path is joined at the col. The path on the other side of the fence is followed east to the cairn on the highest point, which is on the north side, just before the corner where there is a boundary stone marked 1865.

PEN PUMLUMON ARWYSTLI

Walk north-east for about quarter of a mile aiming for another boundary stone on the fence corner. You pass above the source of the River Wye, which though close is quite a detour to visit as it is some 130ft lower. This next stone is marked 1865 WWW which stands for Watkin Williams Wynn. The Wynns owned land for 50 miles north of here and lived at Wynnstay Park, Ruabon. Continue along the ridge for another mile to the east, using a fence and the boundary stones as a guide in poor visibility. The summit is only a few yards to the west of the fence; two large ancient cairns compete for the highest position on the grassy top, with the one to the west winning. They have both been scooped out in the centre.

For the quickest return to the reservoir retrace your steps nearly to the last summit, then descend north-west to Llyn Llygad Rheidol to join the good track which leads gently down past two small lakes to meet the road in a couple of miles. However in good conditions it is well worth continuing north along the ridge to the source of the River Severn and returning through the wild and remote Hengwm valley. Forestry Commission waymarks follow the top edge of the forest to a gate at the forest corner. Continue in the same direction following a fence on the left along the ridge north for another mile to the second of the two little pools, where a fence joins from the west. The source of the River Severn is just over to the east and behind stand the two huge Bronze Age burial cairns, Carn Biga, which appear not to have been excavated.

Return to the ridge and following the fence west descend gradually to the remote upper reaches of the Afon Hengwm. This is a very desolate and wild valley, once populated, its vast boggy wastes are now deserted. Follow the swampy south bank of the river keeping as high as possible in an impossible endeavour to keep your feet dry, to a ruined farmstead at the foot of Cwm Gwerin. After crossing the stream the going gets easier with the suggestion of a track to follow which gradually improves to join the road end above Maesnant, an outdoor pursuits centre. It is then nearly a mile back along the unfenced road to the starting point.

WALK 11.2 PEN Y GARN

SUMMITS:	Pen y Garn	2001ft (610m)
DISTANCE:	6 miles	
ASCENT:	910 feet	
MAPS:	OS Landranger sheet 135, Explorer 213	
STARTING POINT:	(135-765756) The Ystwyth Forest by the Arch on the B4574, 2 miles south-east of Devil's Bridge. Forestry Commission car park, toilets.	

Immediately to the south of Pumlumon is an area of upland moor and forest in the midst of which is the isolated summit of Pen y Garn. To the west the Ystwyth Forest blankets the ground, to the south and east the land is very boggy, while to the north there is both bog and forest. The chosen approach through the forest follows a right of way which is now unfortunately a main, very dusty forest road. Though rather dull, this delivers a dry-shod walker to just beneath the summit after two and a half miles of a steady uphill plod. The descent is much more attractive and follows old ways through the forest. If time is short, a quick raid on the summit can be made from the minor road to the south at 135-784753, where there is room to park a couple of cars.

Spanning the B4574, an old turnpike road, just by the Forestry Commission car park is a huge masonry arch. This was erected in 1810 by Thomas Johnes to commemorate the Golden Jubilee of George III. Johnes planted over 4,000,000 trees here between 1796 and 1813, resolving to restore and make use of an area which had been destroyed by mining. He lived in nearby Cwmystwyth, a beautiful valley scarred by lead mining.

The Arch, Devil's Bridge

The start of the walk is only two miles from Devil's Bridge where upon payment of a fee you can visit the three bridges. The lowest bridge is medieval, the middle bridge eighteenth century and the highest bridge, which is the one in use today, nineteenth century. There is also an interesting nature trail.

Devil's Bridge is also the terminus of the Vale of Rheidol, Lein Fach, narrow-gauge railway which was opened in 1902 to carry lead, timber and passengers the 11¾ miles to Aberystwyth. It was the last steam railway owned by British Rail.

ROUTE DESCRIPTION

PEN Y GARN *(Top of the Cairn)*

Take the higher of the two roads from the car park and after quarter of a mile, just beyond the crossroads, fork right and continue up the main track. In a mile where a road joins from the left keep straight on, then fork left at both of the next two junctions where roads go off downhill. The forest edge is reached in a further three-quarters of a mile. The track climbs steadily all the way and does not make for exciting walking, but there are pleasant glimpses of Cwmystwyth. At the edge of the forest a gate leads onto the open hillside and it is only 300ft of ascent over grass to the summit. An OS trig point stands

185

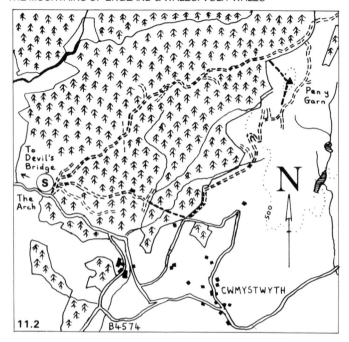

beside a windshelter, hollowed from an ancient cairn, in a commanding position above the forest on the edge of the rather boggy moor. There are views towards Pumlumon and Cadair Idris to the north.

To descend continue south along the ridge for quarter of a mile to the col. Turn right through a gate and immediately fork left to take the track which zigzags down the hill by a little wood to an old quarry. Fork right keeping to the main track passing a series of trial fields labelled with different formulae. Where the track enters the forest, turn left and follow the edge of the trees to a minor metalled road (the starting point for the short walk). Here a gate leads into the forest and a delightful grassy track is taken, for all too short a way, to a footbridge. Cross a forest road to a second footbridge which has been swept away by a storm; it seems impossible that such a tiny stream could do so much damage. A second forest road is crossed and an old road, whose banks are covered with flowers, is followed through a clearing, past Gelmast Farm, back into the forest. From here it is only quarter of a mile, forking left at a T-junction, to the first crossroads of the walk.

WALK 11.3 GORLLWYN AND DRYGARN FAWR

SUMMITS:	Gorllwyn	2011ft (613m)
	Drygarn Fawr	2103ft (641m)
DISTANCE:	10 miles	
ASCENT:	1550 feet	
MAPS:	OS Landranger sheet 147, Explorer 200	
STARTING POINT:	(147-900616) The west end of the Caban-coch Reservoir, 6 miles south-west of Rhayader. Car park at Llanerch Cawr.	

The hills which surrounded the Elan Valley are wild, desolate and beautiful and the walking hard over rough pathless moorland. We came to this area and sought out the rights of way; they were few and seldom evident on the ground. We didn't know at the time that we need not have worried, public access to the whole of the Elan Valley catchment area is guaranteed by Act of Parliament. Long before the Mass Trespasses and Access Agreements of the Peak District, the local population fought and won the right to roam freely over these hills. This was in 1892 when the first reservoirs were to be constructed and the act gave the right of access to unenclosed land for the purpose of enjoying 'air exercise and recreation'. The land to the south of the Elan Estate passed into the hands of the National Trust in 1984, so that free access now extends over an enormous area. If only this were true of all Britain's mountain regions! Although much of the area is high moorland, only two summits within the estate reach mountain status.

This walk follows the Marchnant, stallion's stream, onto the ridge, a surprisingly easy ascent, with the return along the beautiful valley of the Pant Glas, thus reducing the difficult ridge walking to a minimum. Although on one visit the lower slopes of Gorllwyn were busy with a motley collection of Welsh and English foxhounds enjoying a hunt, the hills are usually very quiet and deserted. The only encounter we have had on the tops in fact was a trio of mountain-bikers on the summit of Drygarn Fawr.

The Caban-coch Reservoir is one of five reservoirs built to supply Birmingham with water. Divided from the adjacent reservoir of Carreg-ddu by a submerged dam topped with a road bridge, water is taken out at the Foel Tower just north of the bridge. From here it flows by gravity all the way to Birmingham, a distance of 73 miles. A fall of 170ft is required, but as the base of the Caban-coch dam is below this, once the water level falls below the submerged dam at the bridge, the Caban-coch water is used to maintain the flow of the River Wye.

Traces of prehistoric man have been found in the area, an ancient road crosses the Cwmdeuddwr Hills and Stone Age implements have been found.

187

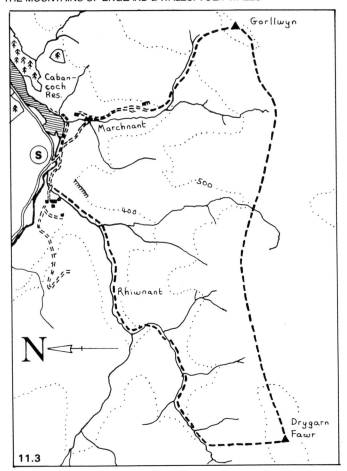

11.3

There are stone circles, standing stones and cairns of the Bronze Age and much later the region was inhabited by the Romans.

If the name Drygarn Fawr means three large cairns, where is the third? The origin of these cairns is a mystery. Although obviously in too good a condition to be anything other than modern, they were constructed sufficiently long ago for much local knowledge to have been lost. The stones themselves are from the original Bronze Age cairns built between 2000 and 1500 BC. A cairn on Drygarn Fawr, which was used as a trigonometrical station in 1851, was rebuilt in 1884 to commemorate the original one, but this was not used again by the OS as their concrete pillar was erected in 1936. The cairns were repaired about 1920, probably to commemorate the coming of age of Captain Evan Thomas of Builth Wells.

ROUTE DESCRIPTION

GORLLWYN *(Above the Grove)*

Cross the Afon Claerddu on the new bridge which stands beside its predecessor, then fork right at the track junction to pass in front of a whitewashed bungalow. After 200 yards the track crosses the Marchnant and then climbs to the left of the stream to some old quarries. The stone from these was used to construct the 184ft high curved dam of the Claerwen Reservoir. This was built from 1946 to 1952 by a firm called Nuttall (no relation to the authors!). Continue following the brook keeping to the left-hand tributary climbing first over tussocky grass on sheep paths and then high above the south bank on easy grassy slopes. When the stream forks, aim south-east for the summit which soon appears ahead. The stone OS trig point is perched on one side of a hollowed-out ancient cairn. On the other side of a peaty depression, 300 yards away to the south-west, is a fine cairn, and a small windshelter, but the automatic weather station is now derelict.

DRYGARN FAWR *(Three Large Cairns)*

A mile and a half of rough pathless walking along the ridge which runs first south-west and then north-west leads to the col between the two tops. Here one of the few paths in this wild area is crossed at Bwlch y Ddau Faen, pass of the two stones. This probably refers to two ancient marker stones long disappeared; a copper axe found here is now in the local museum. A wavering line of concrete boundary posts marked BC (Birmingham Corporation) gives a guide as to the direction to take. From the col it is another 2 miles of real bog-trotting to the spectacular cairns of Drygarn Fawr. It is advisable to take a line to the north of the bwlch to avoid the worst marsh which has been officially tested as knee-deep! About halfway a faint path materialises near the boundary stones and the walking suddenly becomes easier underfoot as the ground rises. The first beehive cairn has a cap of white quartz, but the second, a quarter mile further on, is higher and dwarfs the OS trig point which is set a little way downhill.

To descend, head north over trackless moor to reach the Pant Glas, blue green valley. Although following the stream is easier than the flanking moorland it takes a long time to go a short way as you cross and recross to find the easiest line. After passing a fine waterfall another stream joins from the west and from here it is advisable to stay on the south bank as the

Rhiwnant, hill stream, can be difficult to ford in its lower reaches. High above the stream on its north side runs an old road to the lead mines, but it is not worth making a detour to join this as in places the way has deteriorated to a glutinous bog. Finally climb up from the river to join a main track which leads back to the road and bridge at the start of the walk.

WALK 11.4 THE RADNOR FOREST

SUMMITS:	Bache Hill	2001ft (610m)
	Black Mixen	2133ft (650m)
	Great Rhos	2165ft (660m)
DISTANCE:	9 miles	
ASCENT:	1750 feet	
MAPS:	OS Landranger sheet 148, Explorer 200 & 201	
STARTING POINT:	(148-213610) The village of New Radnor. Parking for a couple of cars at the end of Mutton Dingle. Extra parking by the Cornewall-Lewis memorial.	

Isolated from the other mountain areas in central Wales, the hills of the Radnor Forest rise suddenly from surroundings of lush farmland. This expanse of high moorland covered with heather, cotton grass and bilberry and cut into by attractive steep-sided valleys, has like New Radnor at its foot a quiet and sleepy air. To find three summits over 2000ft is therefore quite a surprise.

The word forest means an unenclosed space for hunting, though the old word now has modern relevance as much land has been taken over by the Forestry Commission. On the border of England and Wales, the place names are a quaint mixture of Welsh and English. Davy Morgan's Dingle lies below Esgairnantau, while Great Creigiau mixes both languages in the same name. To the south lies Water-break-its-neck waterfall, the best falls in Radnorshire. The stream falls 70ft into a gloomy chasm in the forest, but is best visited after a long wet spell as it almost disappears in dry weather. The walk circumnavigates Harley Dingle which is unfortunately used sometimes for ammunition testing, but as all has been quiet on our visits, this in no way detracted from the walk.

The attractive village of New Radnor is laid out in a squared form which dates from the thirteenth century. It was at one time the county town of Radnorshire and once possessed a castle. It was in fact a walled town, but little remains to be seen of these former antiquities save grassy mounds. The castle mound, a splendid vantage point overlooking New Radnor, is the site of a Norman castle which was sacked by Owain Glyndwr in 1401. The most striking thing still to be seen in New Radnor however is the fantastic Victorian memorial to the Right Honourable Sir George Cornewall-Lewis, Baronet, a Whig statesman and scholar who died in 1863. The memorial was partially restored in the Silver Jubilee Year of 1977.

Great Rhos was our last top when completing the Welsh 2000ft summits for the first time. To our friends' surprise we produced a celebratory bottle of wine from the rucksack and drank a toast beside the trig point. The summit, with the standard concrete OS trig point and shrouded by mist with just a hint of drizzle, was reminiscent of so many other almost identical spots. It seemed a fitting end to our exertions and it was somehow appropriate to finish with such a very ordinary sort of a mountain.

ROUTE DESCRIPTION

Black Mixen summit

BACHE HILL *(Small Hill)*
Leave the ancient town of New Radnor by Mutton Dingle, a narrow little lane. After about 200 yards, fork right opposite a small cottage and climb up the unsurfaced road for half a mile to a gate beside a wood. Continuing to climb beside the wood, turn left off the grassy track at the top of the hill into the trees. A little path leads over an old embankment above a dried-up millpond and climbs to join a forest road which continues uphill. About 50 yards after a sharp left-hand bend, turn right along a rougher track, which short cuts the loop in the main forest road, climbing to the top of the forest where the forest road is rejoined. Turn right, passing a farm building; the conical hill to the left is the Whimble. Continue along the track through a gate and at the fork

191

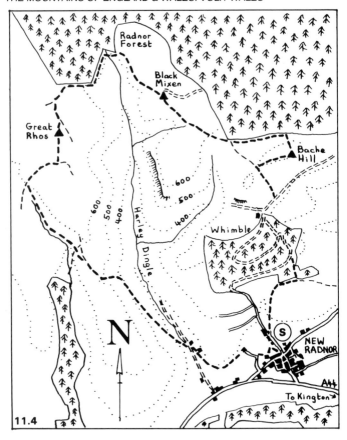

go through the left-hand gate to climb up an old trackway along the edge of an open heather moor, beside a grassy field. A gate at the highest point leads right into a field and the summit of Bache Hill is quarter of a mile away along the ridge. A trig point set on a small mound amidst a sea of heather and bilberry gives excellent views.

BLACK MIXEN *(Black Dunghill - from Old English not Welsh!)*
Descend north over the moor to join the right of way at the edge of the forest.

This leads beside the trees to a gate where it joins the old trackway beside a small pond. The trackway passes through another gate and you leave the forest to climb west on a track that runs along the edge of the Harley Dingle ammunition range, passing a small rocky quarry. To your left is the boggy mound of Great Creigiau, named after the rocky slopes on the western side. Continue along the track to Black Mixen which now sports a new building beside the transmitter mast. The summit is marked by another OS trig point sitting on a small mound where you can look back to Bache Hill and on ahead to Great Rhos.

GREAT RHOS *(Great Moor)*

A small path from the trig point to the left of the buildings leads west to a prominent post, a truncated pole, and from here winds along the edge where you can look across Harley Dingle to Great Rhos on the other side. In about half a mile the path joins the forest edge above Shepherd's Well, a useful spring at the top of the Dingle. Continue beside the forest, with good views of the Great Creigiau and Little Creigiau crags to the left, for another half mile to join a water-eroded Land-rover track from the wood. This runs over the moor beside a fence and after 200 yards, forks left away from the fence. In about another 300 yards a path joins from the right and the OS summit trig point, sitting like the other two on a small mound in the midst of rather boggy heather, is 100 yards away to the south-east. You can look back to the other tops of the walk but the summit is rather flat and it is not a good viewpoint.

Next go south crossing a fence to pick up a faint track in quarter of a mile, which is followed right through cotton grass to a gate. To the left you can see the bulldozed tracks made when fighting the great fire of 1976. On the left is the dry bed of Davy Morgan's Dingle and this should be followed down for quarter of a mile to where a stile crosses the fence on the right. Now climb left onto the open moor to a little alpine path which runs high above the Dingle. Crossing a track, the col between Great Rhos and Fron Hill is reached and then you descend beside an old slate quarry into Harley Dingle. Beyond the gate there is a lovely view across the valley to the Whimble, only marred by a large notice 'WARNING AMMUNITION TESTING takes place in the Harley Valley behind this noticeboard and it is DANGEROUS to leave the bridleroad'. The track continues its gentle descent into the valley. This is one of those rare walks where you seem to go down more than you climb up. Cross the stream at a footbridge and fork left up a metalled road. This soon becomes unsurfaced and leads back through the fields to the houses of New Radnor. At the bed, by a footpath notice and a small gate, stepping-stones begin the path which leads to the church after crossing the town wall. Passing in front of the church the path leads below the castle mound, which gives superb views of the village of New Radnor, to emerge exactly at the end of Mutton Dingle, the starting point.

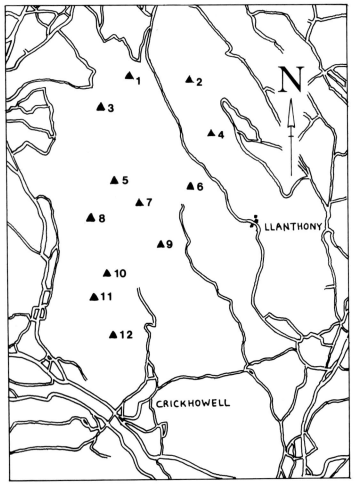

12. THE BLACK MOUNTAINS

CHAPTER 12: THE BLACK MOUNTAINS

TOP	NAME	HEIGHT	GRID REF	WALK No.
1	Twmpa	680m	161-225350 SO	12.1
2	Black Mountain	703m	161-255354 SO	12.1
3	Rhos Dirion	713m	161-211334 SO	12.1
4	Black Mountain South Top	637m	161-267322 SO	12.1
5	Waun Fach	811m	161-216300 SO	12.2
6	Chwarel y Fan	679m	161-259293 SO	12.1
7	Pen y Gadair Fawr	800m	161-229288 SO	12.2
8	Mynydd Llysiau	663m	161-208279 SO	12.2
9	Pen Twyn Mawr	658m	161-242267 SO	12.2
10	Pen Twyn Glas	646m	161-213257 SO	12.2
11	Pen Allt-mawr	719m	161-207243 SO	12.2
12	Pen Cerrig-calch	701m	161-217224 SO	12.2

Ponies on Rhos Dirion

WALK 12.1 THE EASTERN BLACK MOUNTAINS

SUMMITS:	Black Mountain South Top	2090ft (637m)
	Black Mountain	2306ft (703m)
	Twmpa	2231ft (680m)
	Rhos Dirion	2339ft (713m)
	Chwarel y Fan	2228ft (679m)
DISTANCE:	14 miles	
ASCENT:	2400 feet	
MAPS:	OS Landranger sheet 161	
	Explorer OL13 - Brecon Beacons Eastern Area	
STARTING		
POINT:	(161-255314) Capel-y-ffin, 6 miles south of Hay-on-Wye. Limited car parking on the roadside.	

The Black Mountains at the eastern end of the Brecon Beacons National Park provide, after an initial steep ascent, miles of easy walking on high level ridges. The Offa's Dyke path, which follows the easternmost of these ridges along the boundary between Wales and England, is a very popular long distance walk, but few of the people met will be concerned with the summits. In fact the summits are very much incidental in this area, points which are arithmetically superior to their surroundings, but often mere swellings of grass and heather moorland, undistinguished in almost all other respects. The chief attractions are the remarkably steep escarpment edges. In wet conditions the easy walking quickly deteriorates to a peaty mire and the ridges are best kept for dry days.

Capel-y-ffin, chapel on the boundary, lies on the boundary of the old counties of Monmouthshire and Breconshire, high in the Vale of Ewyas on the only road which crosses the Black Mountains. The summit of this road, which rises to 1778ft, is called the Gospel Pass, Bwlch yr Efengyl. The name probably dates from the Crusades when in 1118 Archbishop Baldwin and the Archdeacon of Brecon preached and campaigned here.

Halfway up the 11-mile long valley are the ruins of the twelfth-century Llanthony Priory, but Capel-y-ffin also once had a monastery of its own. This was built in 1870 by Joseph Lyne, an Anglican clergyman. Known as Father Ignatius he founded his own community of Benedictine monks and lived here until his death in 1908. After this the monastery declined and the church, which had never been completed, was soon in a dangerous condition. The rest of the buildings have since had a variety of uses, the gaunt ruins still stand among the trees and, if prominent notices can be believed, are still dangerous.

This is Kilvert Country, The Reverend Francis Kilvert kept an extensive diary giving us a daily picture of country life in Victorian times. He was curate at Clyro near Hay-on-Wye, just north of the Black Mountains, from 1865 to 1872, and his writings during this time mention visits to local places. Kilvert went to Capel-y-ffin in 1870. He was surprised to find the monks doing heavy manual work on a hot day dressed in long black cloaks and remarked "perhaps they did not take off their habits when at work because they had nothing under". Later he made friends with Father Ignatius and was invited to lay a foundation stone in the wall of the new monastery they were building. He describes Capel-y-ffin as "the old chapel short stout and boxy with its little bell turret (the whole building reminded one of an owl), the quiet peaceful chapel yard shaded by seven great solemn yews, the chapel house, a farm house over the way, and the Great Honddu brook crossing the road and crossed in turn by the stone foot bridge". He was much taken by the "buxom

Capel-y-ffin

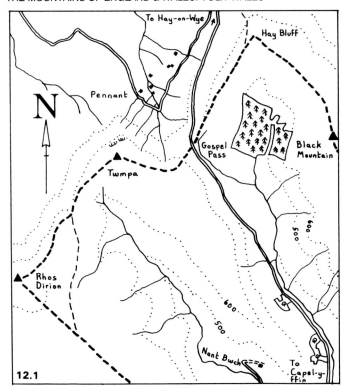

12.1

comely wholesome girl with fair hair, rosy face, blue eyes, and fair clear skin stood washing at a tub in the sunshine, up to the elbows of her round white lusty arms in soapsuds". The little Church in Wales looks much the same today. The small whitewashed Baptist chapel on the other side of the brook was built in 1762.

ROUTE DESCRIPTION

BLACK MOUNTAIN SOUTH TOP
A waymarked lane to the right of the church crosses the Afon Honddu and leads past the chapel to a house called Blaenau. Passing the house, the green lane continues down the valley to become indistinct in the fields, but the waymarks carry on over stiles to a ford where the lane reappears. After

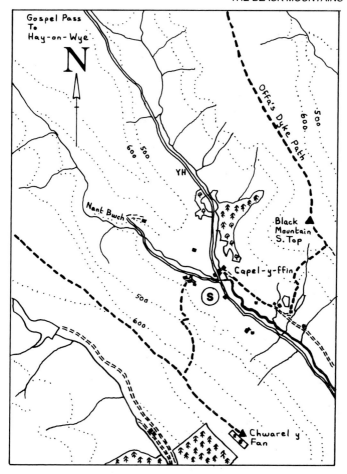

passing Ty'r-onen, house of the ash, the path leads up onto the open hillside to meet the Offa's Dyke Path which follows the ridge. Turn left to the first top, the summit of tussocky grass and heather is marked with a small cairn just to the left of the path.

Hay Bluff

BLACK MOUNTAIN
Continuing along the Offa's Dyke Path it descends gently for just 50ft then, after a couple of miles of easy ascent, the newly flagged path passes over this second undistinguished top. There are pleasant views in all directions, but nothing to mark the summit.

LORD HEREFORD'S KNOB or TWMPA *(Mound)*
Shortly after, the Offa's Dyke Path slides off down the side of the ridge to head for Hay-on-Wye. Continuing however along the ridge, the ground below falls steeply away and the path continues to the trig point on Hay Bluff. This is the most impressive top so far but unfortunately with only 35ft of ascent it fails to qualify as a mountain. The scenery from here to the next trig point is very fine as the path follows the edge of the escarpment south-west all the way with views over the Wye valley to the Cambrian Mountains and the Radnor Forest. Descend to cross the road at the Gospel Pass and then it is a climb of less than 500ft on a good path to the top of Twmpa. The neat grassy summit has a small cairn of flat stones and many small depressions which provide good

shelter from the wind. The escarpment is a popular place for gliders and hang-gliders which tack to and fro in the upcurrents and also more unusually by paragliders, who fly their parachutes from the edges.

RHOS DIRION *(Gentle Moor)*
Continue to follow the path along the edge to this next summit which has a white painted OS trig point set a little back from the edge. A short stroll to the lip of the escarpment gives panoramic views.

CHWAREL Y FAN *(Quarry Beacon)*
Leaving the edge now turn left and follow the main path south-east over Twyn Talycefn, which although not a top has a cairn of which other summits would be proud. The ridge is narrower than the extensive flat moor of the Offa's Dyke ridge and hence gives better views. The odd boundary stone is passed and soon Grwyne Fawr Reservoir appears below to the right. After four miles, at a beehive-shaped cairn, the ridge narrows and rises to a rocky rib above the Mynydd Du Forest. A large cairn marks the highest point on this final summit which has in the past been quarried in a small way.

The moor below is rough and the hillside steep, so retrace your steps for three-quarters of a mile to the beehive cairn, this is no hardship as it is the best ridge section on the walk. A good path north zigzags down over the cliffs into the Vale of Ewyas to join a lane. To the right are the monastery ruins and on joining the road there is a shrine in memory of Father Ignatius. Turn right down the lane back into Capel-y-ffin.

WALK 12.2 THE WESTERN BLACK MOUNTAINS

SUMMITS:	Pen Cerrig-calch	2300ft (701m)
	Pen Allt-mawr	2359ft (719m)
	Pen Twyn Glas	2119ft (646m)
	Mynydd Llysiau	2175ft (663m)
	Waun Fach	2661ft (811m)
	Pen y Gadair Fawr	2625ft (800m)
	Pen Twyn Mawr	2159ft (658m)
DISTANCE:	13½ miles	
ASCENT:	2850 feet	
MAPS:	OS Landranger sheet 161	
	Explorer OL13 - Brecon Beacons Eastern Area	
STARTING POINT:	(161-234229) A small car park at the apex of a hairpin bend 3 miles up the minor road running north from Crickhowell.	

Unlike the eastern summits of the Black Mountains which are crossed by the Gospel Pass, there is no road to intrude upon the wildness of the western area. The road from Llanbedr penetrates as far as the Hermitage, but beyond there is only the mountains, though at one time the pass appears to have been in very active use from the ancient tracks which converge upon it. Rhiw Trumau is an ancient trackway from Castell Dinas in the Rhiangoll valley, but the broad and gently graded track which crosses the bwlch into the Grwyne Fechan valley has an altogether more unusual explanation. The track, which would obviously take a horse and carriage, is reputed to have been constructed by the wealthy landowner John Macnamara in the eighteenth century in order to visit his mistress who was secreted at the Hermitage. This house was part of the estate which Macnamara is supposed to have won gambling.

The character of the area is similar in many ways to the eastern area with long ridges undulating over summits which rise relatively little above the general level. The finest summit is perhaps the first one, Pen Cerrig-calch, whose top differs from the rest of the range in having an extensive area of limestone which contrasts dramatically with the surrounding black peat. The tops are not otherwise themselves notable, but once on the ridge, mile after mile of easy walking on generally good paths can be enjoyed. In fact for some

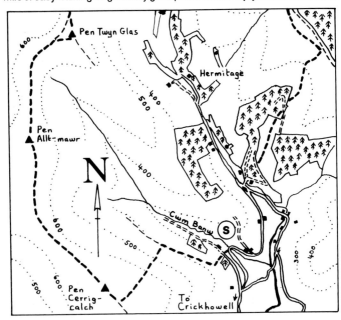

nine miles the walk remains above 2000ft. The area is by no means overrun and on our visits here we have encountered more horses than people. The ponies are not however, as might be thought, wild, but are turned out to graze and roam freely over the hills.

Although the Reverend Francis Kilvert, whose diary has become a classic, climbed Cadair Idris, he does not appear to have walked much upon his local mountains preferring to admire them from a distance.

"The Black Mountains were invisible, being wrapped in clouds, and I saw one very white brilliant dazzling cloud where the mountains ought to have been. This cloud grew more white and dazzling every moment, till a clearer burst of sunlight scattered the mists and revealed the truth. This brilliant white cloud that I had been looking and wondering at was the mountain in snow. The last cloud and mist rolled away over the mountain tops and the mountains stood up in the

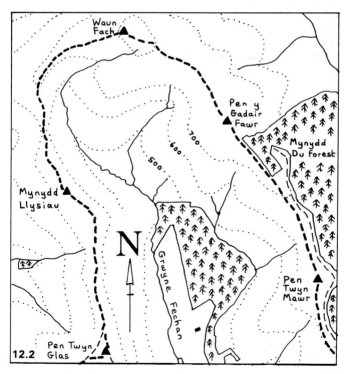

clear blue heaven, a long rampart line of dazzling glittering snow so as no fuller on earth can white them. I stood rooted to the ground, struck with amazement and overwhelmed at the extraordinary splendour of this marvellous spectacle. I never saw anything to equal it I think, even among the high Alps."

ROUTE DESCRIPTION

PEN CERRIG-CALCH *(Limestone Head)*

Of two permissive footpaths which start from the car park, take the one on the south side of the stream and climb steeply up the field. Crossing the lane at the stiles, carry straight on beside the wood and at its top climb straight ahead to join a path which slants right up the hill. This gains height steadily until it levels out by a prominent hawthorn tree. Leave the path now to tackle the steep bracken and heather-covered slopes direct. Rocks and bilberry follow in a climb of about 600ft, but it is the only tough ascent of the day and soon the angle eases to grassy slopes. Beyond are the brilliant white rocks of the summit. Climb up through the stones and after crossing an area of black peat, the OS trig point is soon reached. A few yards to the north is a hollowed-out ancient cairn. To the west lie the Brecon Beacons while to the south-east is the striking cone of the Sugar Loaf.

PEN ALLT-MAWR *(Big Hill End)*

A clear path can now be followed along the ridge, descending over a little outcropping limestone cliff. The path keeps to the right of the ridge, looking down on the head of Cwm Banw and in about a mile and half the OS trig point at the northern end of Pen Allt-mawr is reached. This is situated in the middle of the scattered remains of an ancient cairn whose remnants have been used to construct a windshelter. Across the Rhiangoll valley to the west are the lower summits of Mynydd Troed and Mynydd Llangorse.

PEN TWYN GLAS *(Green Hill Head)*

Descending steeply to the right of the rocky snout, a clear path continues to round the head of Cwm Banw. It is all too easy to miss the next summit as it is not crossed by the main path. About a mile after Pen Allt-mawr a faint path diverges to the right to lead you to the top which is grassy and with a cairn, although a slightly lower bump just to the south has a boundary stone on its top.

MYNYDD LLYSIAU *(Herb Mountain)*

Three hundred yards further north a slight rise is crowned with what appears to be a pair of gravestones. These are in fact boundary stones and are marked with the names of Mrs Macnamara 1811 and DINAS Sir J. Bailey Bart MP 1847. The Macnamaras owned much of the land around here in the mid 1800s.

Waun Fach from the summit of Pen Twyn Mawr

The path runs north for a mile and then bends round north-west following the ridge and climbing almost imperceptibly to the summit of Mynydd Llysiau, a long broad grassy ridge. The unmarked spot height of 663m is just beyond a cairn which has been daubed with paint. The habit of marking cairns with multi-coloured splashes of paint is very much a local aberration which is as unnecessary as it is unsightly.To the right is the Grwyne Fechan valley.

WAUN FACH *(Little Moor)*

Half a mile north, the narrow col is crossed by Macnamara's road, the grassy track now little used. Straight ahead appears to be a fine summit, but Pen Trumau when reached turns out to be only the end of the ridge from Waun Fach and not a separate top at all. The path now climbs more gradually, curling round the edge with extensive views over towards Talgarth on the plain, until Waun Fach is reached. At one time there was an OS trig point on this wet peaty top, but only the concrete plinth remains. The brass dome on it is the OS mark. Trig points, or pillars, are gradually becoming a thing of the past as the OS now rely mainly on a satellite positioning system and as trig points are destroyed by natural (or unnatural!) agencies, they are not being replaced. There is a small insignificant cairn beside the plinth. The surrounding area is flat for some distance in all directions and so proves a poor viewpoint. To the south-east the boggy moorland stretches away and the top of Pen y Gadair Fawr peeps above the skyline, while just east of the summit there is a ruined fence enclosing a small artificial pond in the centre of which is a rain gauge.

PEN Y GADAIR FAWR *(Head of the Great Chair)*

Heading south-east there is little sign of a path at first, but soon a line appears and Pen y Gadair Fawr is reached in a mile after crossing a peaty section. There is a cairn on the grassy summit and from here you can identify all the other 2000ft summits of the Black Mountains.

PEN TWYN MAWR *(Great Hill Top)*

It is about a mile and half to the last top on a much clearer path which runs at first beside a forest of stunted pines and then continues to make a beeline for the top across the grassy moor while the forest recedes to the left. There is a cairn with some painted rocks on the flat, grassy top. As well as the Sugar Loaf straight ahead, you can just glimpse the Table Mountain to the right looking quite diminutive from here.

Continue on the path for about a mile to the col where there is a cairn. Turn right downhill and stumble through the heather by a line of old shooting butts until a good path on the lower bracken slopes eases the descent to the forest road. Go straight across and then left beside the wall through a gloomy tunnel of forest to emerge into fields beyond. The right of way, which continues in the same line, is overgrown and it is easier to walk beside it following the field boundary until the forest is re-entered at a gate. Turn left on the track which follows the forest edge for about 300 yards before it turns sharp right by a magnificent ash tree and descends to Brook Cottage. Turn left to the lane, go straight across up a gravelly track and then left along the road for less than a mile back to the little car park.

Boundary stones on Pen Twyn Glas

The Brecon Beacons from Y Gyrn

CHAPTER 13: THE BRECON BEACONS

TOP	NAME	HEIGHT	GRID REF	WALK No.
1	Garreg Lwyd	616m	160-740179 SN	13.7
2	Garreg Las	635m	160-777203 SN	13.6
3	Picws Du	749m	160-812219 SN	13.6
4	Fan Brycheiniog	802m	160-825218 SN	13.6
5	Fan Hir	761m	160-831209 SN	13.6
6	Fan Gyhirych	725m	160-880190 SN	13.5
7	Fan Fraith	668m	160-887183 SN	13.5
8	Fan Nedd	663m	160-913184 SN	13.5
9	Fan Llia	632m	160-938186 SN	13.5
10	Fan Frynych	629m	160-958228 SN	13.4
11	Craig Cerrig-gleisiad	629m	160-961218 SN	13.4
12	Fan Fawr	734m	160-970193 SN	13.4
13	Y Gyrn	619m	160-989216 SN	13.4
14	Corn Du	873m	160-007213 SO	13.1
15	Pen y Fan	886m	160-012216 SO	13.1
16	Cribyn	795m	160-023213 SO	13.1
17	Fan y Big	719m	160-037207 SO	13.1
18	Bwlch y Ddwyallt	754m	160-055203 SO	13.2
19	Waun Rydd	769m	160-062206 SO	13.2
20	Allt Lwyd	654m	160-079189 SO	13.2
21	Cefn yr Ystrad	617m	160-087137 SO	13.3
22	Waun Lefrith	677m	160-798215 SN	13.6

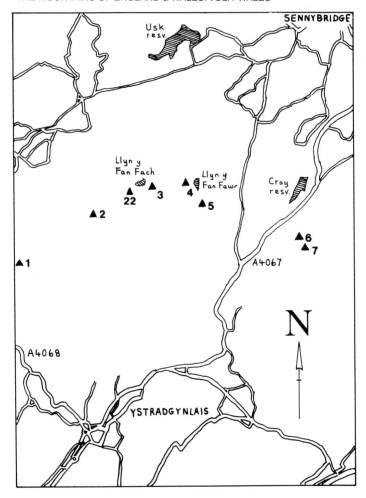

13 WEST. THE BRECON BEACONS

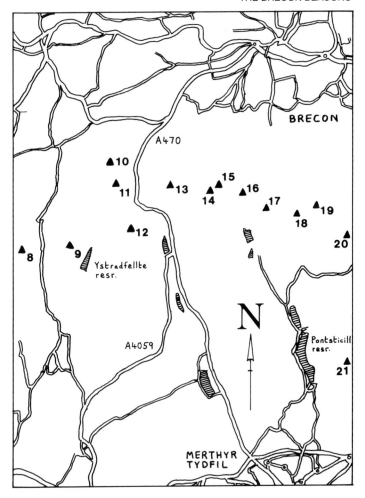

13 EAST. THE BRECON BEACONS

WALK 13.1 THE BRECON BEACONS

SUMMITS:	Corn Du	2864ft (873m)
	Pen y Fan	2907ft (886m)
	Cribyn	2608ft (795m)
	Fan y Big	2359ft (719m)
DISTANCE:	8¹/₂ miles	
ASCENT:	2550 feet	
MAPS:	OS Landranger sheet 160	
	Explorer OL12 - Brecon Beacons Western Area	
STARTING POINT:	(160-036171) Blaen Taf Fechan Forestry Commission car park beside the road to the Neuadd Reservoirs 4 miles north of Pontsticill.	

Although the name more properly belongs to the mountains south of Brecon, the range of summits which stretches over 20 miles across South Wales is generally referred to as the Brecon Beacons. The boundary of the National Park goes even further to take in the Black Mountains to the east, but these have been given a chapter of their own. The central summits of the Beacons belong to an area known as Fforest Fawr, while the westernmost summits are known collectively and also rather confusingly as Black Mountain.

The shape of the hills is largely determined by the rock, old red sandstone, which produces rounded hills, but also dramatically steep escarpment edges. Walking is generally easy, but in winter the conditions can be very wild with shelter and safety many miles distant.

Pen y Fan is the highest of the mountains in the Beacons, reaching almost to 3000ft. From the west the striking and easily identified outline of Corn Du and Pen y Fan may encourage an ascent from this side, but not only is this a dull trudge enlivened only by the Tommy Jones memorial and the final steep slopes of Corn Du but also so many people make the ascent from the Storey Arms that the path is becoming badly worn. Much to be preferred is the approach from the south which makes a fine horseshoe ridge walk taking in a total of four summits. There is the bonus of no tiresome road walking on the return journey as the ridge curves neatly round almost back to the starting point.

Thick damp misty conditions are far from ideal on any mountain, but we could not reasonably expect the perfect weather of a previous visit to be repeated. There was little to be seen of the Beacons as we passed the nearly dry Lower Neuadd Reservoir. Completed in 1884 to provide water to Merthyr Tydfil it was failing in its purpose with only a small guilty-looking puddle in the

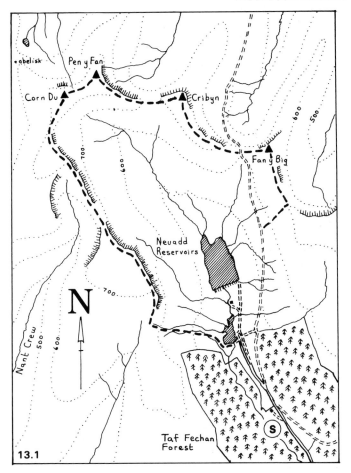

13.1

bottom. The walk along the Graig Fan Ddu ridge confirmed early impressions, there was nothing to see except a few feet of muddy path. Suddenly, and in a matter of a few minutes, the scene was transformed. First a few holes were torn, through which blue sky and racing clouds appeared, then the entire grey world vanished and the mountains seemed to stretch away to the horizon. Once again we were in luck and the tops stayed out of the clouds for the rest of the day. Admittedly there are days which turn out to be wet and nasty in the extreme, but we have had some marvellous walks on days when just to get out of the car seemed foolhardy!

ROUTE DESCRIPTION

CORN DU *(Black Horn)*

Take the tarmac road to the Lower Neuadd Reservoir and in a few yards the Brecon Beacons come into view ahead. In half a mile the road arrives at iron gates. Go through, passing the sign saying 'No unauthorised entry' (it's a public right of way), descend left to a footbridge across the leat and walk across the dam to a stile. A path ascends rightwards across the boggy lower slopes following beside a stream then steeply up to the broad ridge. On reaching the ridge turn right on a clear path along the edge of Graig Fan Ddu. Gradually the ridge narrows and now the views into the wide Taf Fechan valley on the right are augmented by those into the narrow Cwm Crew on the left. After two miles of easy walking with the Brecon Beacons ahead Bwlch Duwynt is reached with a bright red eroded path ascending Corn Du ahead. A short climb, with a natural stone staircase up the old red sandstone at the steepest bit and the flattish summit area is soon attained with a cairn, a collapsed pile of stones, at the far end. Straight ahead is Brecon and tucked in at the base of the near vertical northern slope is Llyn Cwm Lwch. Pen y Fan, Cribyn and Fan y Big are of course the closest eastward summits, and westward the nearest is the apparently flat moor of Y Gyrn. The middle distance westward comprises Fan Fawr, Craig Cerrig-gleisiad with its nature reserve, and Fan Frynych, while far out to the west Garreg Lwyd, the westernmost 2000ft summit in the Brecon Beacons, can be seen between the flanking summits of Fan Hir and Fan Gyhirych.

PEN Y FAN *(Top of the Beacon)*

It is a broad ruddy highway that leads to Pen y Fan and not much more than 100ft of ascent to the highest of the Brecon Beacons. The OS trig point is no more and the summit is now topped by a large, flat cairn. The National Trust owns the central summits of the Brecon Beacons, some 8192 acres, and this area round Pen y Fan was gifted to the Trust by the Eagle Star Insurance Company in 1965.

CRIBYN *(The Summit)*

Descending south-east from Pen y Fan on a good path, the sandstone blocks scattered about are so regular in shape that they might be thought to be offcuts from a stonemason. Ahead the continuously steep pyramidal north face of Cribyn looks as though combed by a giant comb. Pen y Fan too is streaked with gullies, which are incised deeper than those on Cribyn. An ascent of about 400ft up the steep grassy slope, which shows less evidence

Pen y Fan from Cribyn

of erosion, brings you to the pointed stony top where there is a low untidy cairn of sandstone blocks. Almost due north the long ridge of Bryn Teg, fair hill, descends towards Brecon about five miles away.

FAN Y BIG *(Beak Beacon)*
The continuation to Fan y Big is down Cribyn's third ridge, heading south and then curling round above the head of Cwm Cynwyn to descend to the major highway crossing Bwlch ar y Fan. This broad track is reputed to be of Roman origin. The summit of Fan y Big is rather different from the previous tops as it is not a peak, but the end of a ridge, and were it not for the Ordnance Survey spot height at the northern end, the exact position of the top might be in doubt. Although there is no cairn, being surrounded on three sides by spectacular drops is distinction enough. A rocky platform high above the valley gives impressive photographs. The three tops of Corn Du, Pen y Fan and Cribyn now lies to the west in a neat row.

Go south along the ridge for about half a mile and then slant down to join the Roman road from the bwlch. A mile and a half of gentle downhill walk remains, with the four summits filling the skyline when you look back up the valley.

WALK 13.2 ALLT LWYD AND WAUN RYDD

SUMMITS:	Allt Lwyd	2146ft (654m)
	Waun Rydd	2523ft (769m)
	Bwlch y Ddwyallt	2474ft (754m)
DISTANCE:	7 miles	
ASCENT:	2050 feet	
MAPS:	OS Landranger sheet 160 & 161	
	Explorer OL12 - Brecon Beacons Western Area	
STARTING POINT:	(161-100197) The minor road to the west of the Talybont Reservoir 2 miles south of Talybont-on-Usk. Car park beside the reservoir.	

To the east of Pen y Fan and the other well-known summits of the Beacons the high ground of peaty moorland continues for a further five miles, all above 2000ft, until the final grassy slopes which drop to the shores of the Talybont Reservoir. This reservoir, which was finished in 1938, provides Newport with water which is purified in the filter house just below the dam, then piped directly to the mains. After the Second World War the surrounding land was leased to the Forestry Commission and the trees were planted from 1952 to 1963. A local nature reserve was created in 1975 which attracts many varieties of birds.

Carn Pica is the prominent cairn at the end of Waun Rydd on the edge of the final drop from the high ground, but the first objective is Allt Lwyd, a spur descending from Waun Rydd. Although the summit is undistinguished, we spent rather longer than expected sitting on its top one October. The reason for this devotion was a most vicious hailstorm. Determined to complete these summits we were reluctant to retreat, but further progress was painful if not impossible until the storm had passed.

ROUTE DESCRIPTION

ALLT LWYD *(Grey Hill)*

Go up the metalled forest road opposite the car park for a short way and when the road bends left take the waymarked footpath, a broad green lane, up through the fields to a stile. Climb to another stile at the corner of the Talybont Forest and then, continuing ever upwards, ascend the grassy slopes to the first summit of the walk where there is a little cairn with an upright stone in the centre. This grassy top has extensive views over to the Black Mountains and you can clearly see Carn Pica and the descent route on the other side of the Nant Tarthwynni.

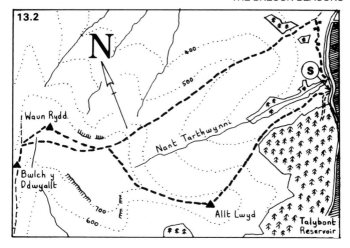

BWLCH Y DDWYALLT *(Two Hills Col)*

It is only 300ft of ascent now up onto the plateau ahead, and all the hard work of the day has been done. The narrow grassy ridge climbs to the flat moorland above and a faint path leads north-west to a cairn, once the site of a trig point, on the main path. Leaving Waun Rydd for the return journey, turn left and descend gently along a rather boggy path for half a mile to a meeting of the ways at the bwlch. Follow the good path which curls round high above Cwm Cwareli to the summit, a stony patch just to the left of the path before some isolated prominent peat hags. The much higher Brecon Beacons with their long ridge lie to the west and the county town of Brecon nestles in the valley below to the north.

WAUN RYDD *(Free Moorland)*

The final summit is clearly in view, a small pimple to the right of a notch in the skyline to the north-east but you have to memorise its position for on retracing your steps to the col it vanishes. From the col head east using sheep tracks to reach the summit cairn a quarter of a mile away. In good visibility the Black Mountains can be seen beyond Llangorse Lake.

A narrow path leads back above the glacial cirque of Craig Pwllfa to the cairn visited on the outward journey, but this time keep to the main path and go east to Carn Pica. This is a magnificent 10ft high cairn of modern origin and a splendid viewpoint. From here the path drops over the red jumbled rocks at the end of the ridge, over Twyn Du, black knoll, then back down into the valley on a broad grassy path through the bracken heading for the dam of the

The ascent of Allt Lwyd

Talybont Reservoir. Keeping to the right of a wall and a wood join a green lane which runs beside a stream. After a rocky section on the path go through a gateway to the right and follow the old track which passes to the left of a barn high above the main road and on to the ruined Berthlwyd-fach farmhouse. Keeping behind the buildings, go through a couple of gates and then slant downhill to another gate to join the line of the old road which flanked by tree stumps, leads to a gate onto the main road by the Nant Tarthwynni. Notice the tank traps which were built for defence in the case of invasion during the Second World War.

WALK 13.3 CEFN YR YSTRAD

SUMMITS:	Cefn yr Ystrad	2024ft (617m)
DISTANCE:	8 miles	
ASCENT:	1050 feet	
MAPS:	OS Landranger sheet 160	
	Explorer OL12 - Brecon Beacons Western Area	

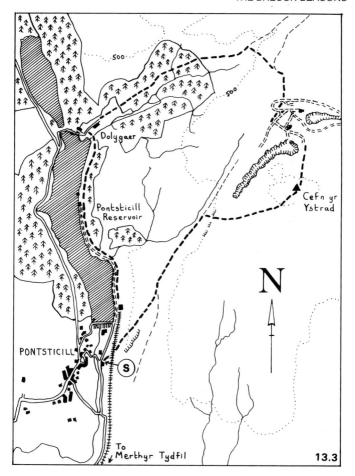

13.3

STARTING
POINT: (160-060113) The road junction below the Pontsticill Reservoir
dam, 2 miles north of Merthyr Tydfil. Parking for a few cars at
the junction, more parking space by the dam.

Pen y Fan from Pontsticill Reservoir

To the east of the Pontsticill Reservoir, above the limestone-rimmed Cwm Criban, is the isolated top of Cefn yr Ystrad. The approach with views across the reservoir is pleasant and the summit, set amid an area of shake holes with two massive ancient cairns is very fine, but sadly to the north the ground has been ravaged by a large working quarry. However once this industrial area has been passed, the walk continues with a tree-lined descent down Cwm Callan to return beside the Pontsticill, bridge of the stile, Reservoir.

Beside the reservoir is the Brecon Mountain Railway, a narrow-gauge line which has been laid on the old Merthyr Tydfil to Brecon railway. The line which opened in 1863 and passed through the highest railway tunnel in Britain at 1313ft, was closed in the drastic cuts of 1962.

The Pontsticill Reservoir makes a welcome addition to the rather gloomy conifers of the Taf Fechan Forest, while the little boats of the Merthyr Tydfil Sailing Club create an attractive picture as they tack to and fro across the water. The crest of the dam was raised in 1988 and the valve house fitted with a gleaming new copper roof. The extensive work closed the road over the dam for six months necessitating a special order from the Secretary of State for Wales.

ROUTE DESCRIPTION

CEFN YR YSTRAD *(Ridge of the Dale)*
From the road junction walk up the road towards the Pontsticill Reservoir dam

for a short way. Just past a cottage turn right through a gate onto an old track which climbs to pass under the railway line. The green lane continues up through the bracken, following the old hedgeline, with good views over the reservoir to the Brecon Beacons. After passing through an ancient iron gate in the wall, continue climbing over the grassy moor in the same direction to join a main track which heads north-east up Cwm Criban. After three-quarters of a mile climb east over the limestone rim of the cwm and then, keeping well to the right of the quarry, head north-east through an area dimpled with shake holes for the summit which, on a clear day, soon appears ahead. The OS trig point is mounted on a large square of concrete and nearby on the humpy summit stand two ancient cairns, Carn Felen and Carn y Bugail. This isolated mountain is a good spot from which to survey the Brecon Beacons to the north-west and the Black Mountains to the north-east.

John on the summit of Cefn yr Ystrad

Descend north between the quarries Cwar yr Ystrad and Cwar yr Hendre which are still being worked. Cross an area of reclaimed ground to the end of a track which passes to the left of a lake to join the concreted mine road. Just beyond is the footpath which heads north cutting across the road at the bends to cross the moor to the head of the Nant Ddu, black stream. Leave the path here and cross the pathless moor westwards to join the bridleway which descends above the Nant yr Ychen to a gate into the Taf Fechan Forest. The broad track through the forest passes the ruins of Blaencallan Farm and then attractively fringed by deciduous trees, continues down Cwm Callan to the Dolygaer Outdoor Pursuits Centre. The now metalled road finally passes underneath a railway bridge where you turn left along the bridleway beside the reservoir for a mile and half. Then the road goes downhill, passing the end of the dam, to the start of the walk.

WALK 13.4 FAN FAWR

SUMMITS:	Fan Frynych	2064ft (629m)
	Craig Cerrig-gleisiad	2064ft (629m)
	Fan Fawr	2408ft (734m)
	Y Gyrn	2031ft (619m)
DISTANCE:	8¹/₂ miles	
ASCENT:	2450 feet	
MAPS:	OS Landranger sheet 160	
	Explorer OL12 - Brecon Beacons Western Area	
STARTING POINT:	(160-972222) Layby and picnic area on the A470, 2 miles north of the Storey Arms.	

The hills to the west of the Storey Arms linked with Y Gyrn, that outlier of the Brecon Beacons, make a pleasant moderate walk. Craig Cerrig-gleisiad and Fan Frynych are part of a National Nature Reserve originated in 1958. Formerly privately managed it has now been purchased by the Nature Conservancy Council. A series of permissive footpaths give access to the summit of Fan Frynych, an area previously denied to walkers. These mountains are the most southerly habitat in Britain of several arctic-alpine plants such as rose root and purple saxifrage which are to be found in this glaciated cirque. The steep old red sandstone cliffs tower above the floor of the cwm upon which there are heaps of glacial moraine.

Y Gyrn, usually bypassed by walkers on their way to Corn Du and Pen y Fan, is open moorland upon which the commoners of the surrounding farms have the right to graze their sheep. High on the skyline leading up to Corn Du,

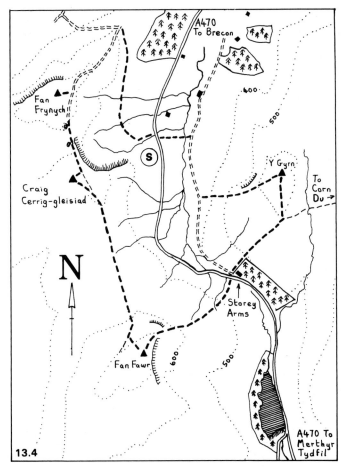

Fan Frynych

Craig Cerrig-gleisiad

N

Fan Fawr

A470 To Brecon

S

Y Gyrn

To Corn Du →

Storey Arms

A470 To Merthyr Tydfil

13.4

the outline of an obelisk can be clearly seen. This monument commemorates the tragic death in 1900 of a 5-year-old local lad, Tommy Jones, who became separated from his father on the way from Brecon Station to visit relatives. The child's body was not found for a month and the obelisk was erected on the spot where he lay.

The A470 was built after 1830 to replace the original turnpike road on the other side of the valley. The old road was still used however by drovers to

223

avoid the tolls on the new road and is known as the old drovers' road.

ROUTE DESCRIPTION

FAN FRYNYCH *(Ox Hill Beacon)*

Follow the waymarked public right of way which starts uphill beside the stream with the cliffs of Craig Cerrig-gleisiad straight ahead and after about 250 yards turn right beside the wall. The clear grassy path goes north for a mile and at a stile joins the permissive path at a hairpin bend, though more recent permissive paths give a shorter route to the summit. The red track goes left, climbing steadily and easily to the summit of Fan Frynych and in fact continues a little further than indicated on the map. The summit with its OS trig point is about 200 yards to the right over the flat moor, which has several small depressions. The views to the west are of the main summits of Fforest

Anne at Tommy Jones memorial

Fawr, while eastwards the distinctive outline of the twin summits of the Brecon Beacons form the skyline. To the north the views are most extensive towards the high ground of mid Wales.

CRAIG CERRIG-GLEISIAD *(Blue Stone Rock)*

Keeping to the permissive path, cross a stile at the bwlch. A short climb brings you to the next top, a grassy mound which is exactly the same height as Fan Frynych, but marked only by a small cairn of sandstone rocks. It is a little to the right of the fence and will be seen clearly ahead as the ascent eases. In mist the top will be found most easily by striking right as soon as flat ground is reached. Ahead the ascent of Fan Fawr appears a considerable undertaking, the mountain looks much steeper than fortunately it proves on closer acquaintance.

FAN FAWR *(Large Beacon)*

The ground ahead is bleak and reminiscent of Derbyshire and Yorkshire moorland, but the dominant bulk of Fan Fawr says this can only be South Wales. The moor, which at first sight looks like a long and difficult crossing, is traversed by a path which heads resolutely for the next top and greatly simplifies the walk. To the right you can see Ystradfellte Reservoir which supplies the people of Neath with water. As the path starts to ascend it is suddenly distracted and veers off to the right. Desert the path now, climbing straight up the hillside over rough grassy slopes. The Ordnance Survey, who elsewhere have usually chosen summits for their columns, have forsaken the top of Fan Fawr and set up their concrete pillar nearly half a mile to the south-west. Perhaps the views are better there, but the true summit has only a small scraped-together pile of sandstone blocks to celebrate its status. To the south-east is seen the chain of three reservoirs running down the Taf Valley which supply Cardiff with water, eastwards is Corn Du, while just peeping out from the mountain's lower slopes is the Storey Arms.

Y GYRN *(The Cairn)*

Leaving Fan Fawr by its north-east ridge, avoiding the precipitous slopes on either hand, a path goes down towards the Storey Arms. This was named after Storey Maskelyne, a local landowner, not alas a hostelry as its name suggests, but one of the ubiquitous outdoor pursuits centres. Cross the road and join the highway to the Brecon Beacons. A steady and rather boggy climb eases after about 300ft of ascent and straight ahead is the striking profile of Corn Du with its curling lip. On the skyline to the left is the outline of Tommy Jones' memorial. Soon the shoulder of Y Gyrn is reached where the main path starts to go gradually downhill. Turn left now to follow the broad ridge on a narrow path heading for a ladder stile on the skyline. On nearing the stile it proves to be merely a rotten and unnecessary remnant without treads, but it serves a useful function still as the summit is only a few yards further along the fence marked by a small pile of sandstone blocks on a peaty tussock. The view is dominated to the east by Corn Du and Pen y Fan.

Now head roughly west across the pathless moor and descend the steep hillside, whose lower slopes are bracken-covered, to a small gate onto the old drovers' road where it enters the National Trust estate of Blaenglyn, head of the glen. Turn right on the track and follow it for about half a mile until a sign points the way over a gate to the youth hostel. 'Please follow footpath', it admonishes, but this is difficult as there is no sign of one. A gateway on the far side of the field leads to the footbridge, while a direct ascent of the field beyond brings you to a stone stile back onto the main road almost opposite the starting point.

WALK 13.5 FAN LLIA TO FAN GYHIRYCH

SUMMITS:	Fan Llia	2073ft (632m)
	Fan Nedd	2175ft (663m)
	Fan Fraith	2192ft (668m)
	Fan Gyhirych	2379ft (725m)
NOTE:	There is a permissive path over Fan Nedd and Fan Gyhirych. This path is CLOSED during the lambing season from 15 April to 10 May.	
DISTANCE:	16 miles	
ASCENT:	3400 feet	
MAPS:	OS Landranger sheet 160 Explorer OL12 - Brecon Beacons Western Area	
STARTING POINT:	(160-927165) The minor road 2 miles north of Ystradfellte, Blaen Llia Forestry Commission car park.	

These wild moor-like hills of Fforest Fawr (a medieval royal hunting forest) lack the striking steep escarpments both of the Brecon Beacons to the east and Bannau Sir Gaer to the west, but unfrequented hills because of their quiet and solitude have an appeal which the more popular summits cannot offer. The three westernmost summits in the walk, Fan Nedd, Fan Fraith and Fan Gyhirych lie in the Cnewr Estate and for many years a policy of total exclusion operated, but now a permissive path has been established. It is however the decision of the estate not to mark the route which though an excellent idea in principle does make it difficult to keep to the line of the path! A second permissive path crosses the estate via the track of one of the most attractive railway lines in Wales, now disused. The track, which ran to Brecon, is followed by a beautiful and lonely walk through the Ogof Ffynnon Ddu Nature

Maen Llia

Reserve. The final section of the walk is along Sarn Helen, the Roman road which ran from Y Gaer, a Roman fort near Brecon, to another fort at Coelbren.

In 1975 Ogof Ffynnon Ddu, cave of the black spring, was declared a National Nature Reserve. This was formed principally to protect the deepest and one of the longest and best studied cave systems in Britain. Crags, rocky outcrops, pavements and swallow holes are prominent surface features of the reserve. In the northern part a narrow band of carboniferous limestone is exposed, but elsewhere is covered by a millstone grit plateau whose pitted surface hints at the underlying limestone.

As might be expected in a limestone area the rivers have a habit of disappearing underground. The Afon Nedd plunges into a fissure at Pwll-y-rhyd and the Afon Mellte disappears most spectacularly into the huge mouth

227

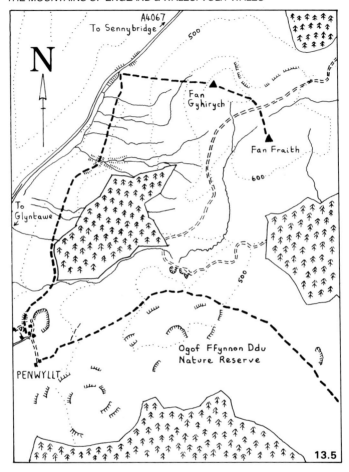

of Porth yr Ogof. In the lower reaches of both rivers there are many beautiful waterfalls.

ROUTE DESCRIPTION

FAN LLIA *(Llia Beacon)*

Cross the Afon Llia at the concrete ford and go left over the right-hand stile

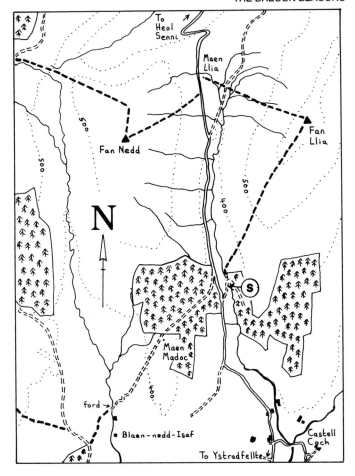

to follow a little track to another stile onto the grassy hillside. Climb steadily north-east across the slope of sheep-cropped turf for a mile to reach a prominent sandstone cairn on the long grassy ridge. From here can be glimpsed the Ystradfellte Reservoir which provides Neath with water. The highest point 400 yards further on is marked by a few stones. To the east stands Fan Fawr with the Brecon Beacons beyond while to the west the steep

229

slopes of Fan Nedd tempt you on.

FAN NEDD *(Neath Beacon)*

Descend easily over grass north-west aiming just to the right of Maen Llia, Llia's stone, to cross Sarn Helen and then over a conveniently placed stile into the field. This Bronze Age monolith is about 12ft high and was probably a marker stone. Cross another stile onto the road and walk left for 150 yards to a ladder stile, (this stile is about 150 yards north of where the footpath is marked on the OS map). A notice gives the conditions to be observed for the use of this permitted path across the Cnewr Estate and the path, on the map only not the ground, makes a beeline south-west for the summit. The ground here is much rougher than on Fan Llia but after 750ft of uphill toil the OS trig point on the grassy top is eventually reached.

FAN FRAITH

Walk north along the ridge, past a roughly constructed windshelter towards a cairn, then head north-west down a spur with views into Blaen Senni. A bit of a path materialises at Bwlch y Duwynt, a waymark on a gatepost points the way west and in just over quarter of a mile you join a main track at a gate. This bright red highway climbs gently to the col between Fan Fraith and Fan Gyhirych where you head left over boggy ground climbing 53ft to the tussocky summit of Fan Fraith which is marked by a few stones.

FAN GYHIRYCH

Return to the track and then head north-west across easy grassy slopes for the OS trig point which stands in the middle of flat moorland. A few yards to the north is an ancient cairn with fine views north over and beyond the Cray Reservoir, which supplies Swansea with water, and west to the Carmarthen Fan hills.

The quickest way back is to retrace your steps, but the continuation described makes a fine wild walk over unfrequented moors. Descend west, steeply at first, to join the A4067 at a stile onto the southern end of a layby just to the left of the tower on the other side of the main road. On reaching the road turn immediately left along the dismantled railway. This shortly re-enters the Cnewr Estate at a gate and another permissive path follows the line of the old railway for a couple of miles of easy walking. The disused track contours round the Tawe valley, below an old tramway, over embankments and across streams. After leaving the estate by a stone quarry, the line disappears under a pile of black gravel. Penwyllt Quarry is still working and huge diggers toil to and fro across a scene of desolation. Passing a sad row of derelict cottages, go to the left of the old Penwyllt, wildtop, railway station where Madam Patti the famous opera singer who lived at nearby Craig-y-nos had her own waiting room. Turn left before the Mountain Rescue Post cottages to enter the Ogof Ffynnon Ddu Nature Reserve at a stile.

After crossing a disused tramway the right of way climbs over the moor passing to the right of a pothole with a padlocked door, then through an area of shake holes. The path widens to a cart track and on its left are a couple of trial enclosures. This area was devastated by fire in 1976 and is now well provided with fire beaters, two of which artistically decorate a small cairn on a prominent knoll. The path runs for one and a half miles through the reserve, roughly parallel to a stone wall on the other side of which a stream disappears at Pwll Byfre to enter the cave system.

The reserve is quitted at a stile and the path continues gently downhill across the heathery moor in the same direction for another two miles. After passing some enclosures and a ruin, turn right onto a red track which leads to a stile at the corner of the forest by Sarn Helen. Turn left through a gate and follow the Roman road downhill to a ford on the left of the farms (if the river is in spate there is a footbridge downstream). Just over half a mile downstream from here the Afon Nedd disappears briefly underground at Pwll-y-rhyd. Sarn Helen now goes uphill passing Maen Madoc, a large standing stone, which has the now illegible Latin inscription 'here lies Dervacus, the son of Justus'. Finally entering the forest the broad track descends to the road close by the car park.

WALK 13.6 CARMARTHEN FAN

SUMMITS:	Fan Hir	2497ft (761m)
	Fan Brycheiniog	2631ft (802m)
	Picws Du	2457ft (749m)
	Waun Lefrith	2221ft (677m)
	Garreg Las	2083ft (635m)
NOTE:	There are some river crossings which could be difficult after heavy rain.	
DISTANCE:	14 miles	
ASCENT:	3150 feet	
MAPS:	OS Landranger sheet 160 Explorer OL12 - Brecon Beacons Western Area	
STARTING POINT:	(160-847169) A4067 Swansea to Brecon road. Parking in the layby on the main road half a mile north of the Dan-yr-Ogof showcaves, opposite the church.	

This remote group of hills, collectively known locally as the Carmarthen Fan, offers fine walking with some five miles of dramatic escarpment edges. The return over the wild moors to the south and west is full of interest, as the area

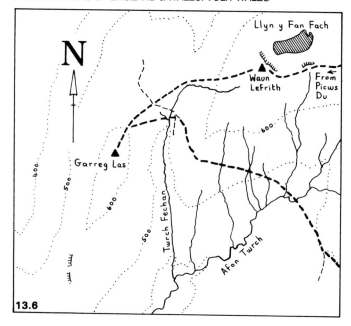

13.6

is liberally sprinkled with shake holes and outcropping limestone.

Beneath the moor is the vast cave system of Dan-yr-Ogof a small part of which is open to the public. There are magnificent stalagmite and stalactite formations in what is advertised as being the longest showcave in Britain and there is also the Cathedral Showcave which has the largest single chamber of any British showcave. The cave was first explored in 1912 by the Morgan brothers. Higher up is Ogof-yr-Esgyrn, cave of the bones, where many human bones were found and this is now also open to the public. The tourist complex which has won many awards also boasts an artificial ski-slope and rather incongruously a Dinosaur Park.

Llyn y Fan Fawr, big lake of the beacon, below Fan Hir, the first summit to be visited, is the source of the Afon Tawe while Llyn y Fan Fach, small lake of the beacon, beneath Bannau Sir Gaer is the legendary home of the Lady of the Lake. She was wooed and won by a local boy who met her when he was minding the cattle. They married on the condition that she would return to the lake is he struck her three times with iron. They had three sons and were very happy, but alas, the inevitable happened as always in fairy stories; in time the husband touched her three times with iron so she disappeared back into the

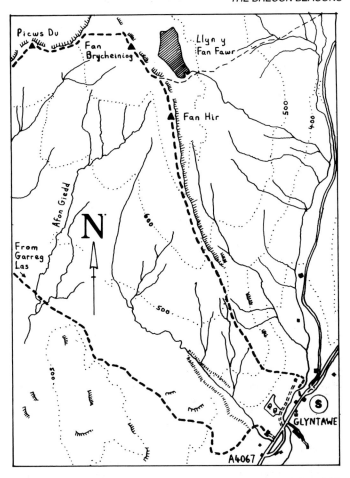

lake with her dowry of cattle and sheep. It is thought that the origins of this story date back to when the Celts arrived in Wales. They used iron and often lived beside lakes, their houses sometimes being raised up on piles above the water.

ROUTE DESCRIPTION

FAN HIR *(Long Beacon)*

Take the footpath opposite the Tafarn-y-Garreg public house, cross the Afon Tawe and follow the river upstream to a gate onto an old lane which is waymarked at the end onto the open hillside. Indistinct minor paths are used to ascend the steep bracken slope until the easier grass of the ridge of Allt Fach is reached. Following a succession of sheep trods a path gradually develops and after passing a stony area the long escarpment, with its fringe of rocks, is followed to the highest point, a grassy top where a few red stones, just the beginnings of a cairn, mark the summit. To the east are the twin-topped Brecon Beacons, below lies Llyn y Fan Fawr while ahead the ridge continues temptingly over Fan Brycheiniog.

FAN BRYCHEINIOG *(Breconshire Beacon)*

Descend to Bwlch Giedd and then it is less than 300ft of ascent to the concrete OS trig point which stands beyond a fine circular windshelter. A second cairned summit of equal height lies quarter of a mile further on round the wide sweep of the escarpment; from this there are extensive views north over the mountains of the Elan Valley to the Pumlumon range.

PICWS DU *(Black Peak)*

After following the escarpment edge for a short way, head west to cut across the neck of the northern promontory for a big descent to Bwlch Blaen-Twrch. The next summit is however lower than the last so it is a short but steep climb to the grassy top which has the remains of an ancient cairn. In the valley to the north is the Usk Reservoir and in the cwm below lies Llyn y Fan Fach surrounded by the cliffs of Bannau Sir Gaer, Carmarthenshire Beacons, of which Picws Du is the highest point.

WAUN LEFRITH *(Milky Moor)*

Continue to follow the edge of the escarpment high above the lake over a minor summit to the large cairn on grassy Waun Lefrith. This new top, proposed by Myrddyn, rises by 17m and from it you can see both the Bristol Channel and Carmarthen Bay.

GARREG LAS *(Blue Stone)*

Descend west over grass to Pen-Rhiw-goch, head of the red track, where a track rises to the south of Carreg Yr Ogof, a small limestone hill with fine rocks which has an OS trig point. Ignoring this summit which is only 585m, turn left on the ridge which is followed south, first over grass, then to the right of the jumbled limestone boulders to the much higher Garreg Las with its two fine ancient cairns, Carnau'r Garreg Las, on the summit. These cairns have been excavated and the northernmost is credited with being the highest.

Return the same way until the worst of the boulders have been passed and you are back on the grass. Then descend east to the head of the Twrch Fechan where a right of way heads south-east all the way back to the starting point. At first there is a main track which crosses the head of the cwm and then swings up and over the ridge ahead. From here you can see that the eastern slopes of Garreg Las are pitted with giant shake holes. The path which leaves the bwlch with great confidence vanishes without trace, so relying on the map it is a wild walk back and a test of navigation to follow the line of the old way. Ford the Afon Twrch, boar river, and then after passing through an area pitted with shake holes cross the Afon Giedd about half a mile above the spot where it vanishes into a swallow hole. The route is full of interest and about two and a half miles from the bwlch, after crossing the Afon Giedd, a good path materialises near the large round pool of Pwl y Cig. From here it is a straightforward matter to follow the improving path for a further couple of miles through the fascinating landscape of shake holes and limestone outcrops. We were interested to find a group of muddy cavers excavating a shake hole in an endeavour to gain access to the major cave system below. Finally after passing some flat limestone rocks with large isolated sandstone blocks sitting on top, the track descends through disused quarries. Ford the River Haffes to a small gate, then walk down an old lane passing to the right of Carreg Haffes Farm to join the main road. If the river is in flood cross the stile before the river and return via the campsite.

Picws Du

WALK 13.7 GARREG LWYD

SUMMITS:	Garreg Lwyd	2021ft (616m)
DISTANCE:	2 miles	
ASCENT:	420 feet	
MAPS:	OS Landranger sheet 160	
	Explorer OL12 - Brecon Beacons Western Area	
STARTING POINT:	(160-732187) Layby and car park at the summit of the A4069 from Brynaman to Llangadog.	

This is the westernmost of the Brecon Beacons and although perhaps neglected compared with the more popular summits further east, it has one of the biggest summit cairns of them all. The A4069, an old turnpike road, snakes its way over the end of the Black Mountain range, rising to a height of 1617ft at Pen Rhiw-wen. George Borrow records passing this way on his walk through South Wales on the evening of November 10th 1854, a dark and misty night. As the complete walk will take at most an hour, it makes a pleasant stroll for a clear evening with the street lights making jewelled patterns in the darkness to the west.

ROUTE DESCRIPTION

GARREG LWYD *(Grey Rock)*

Keeping to the right of the quarries, the ascent is mainly over grass except in the upper part where the rocky bones of the mountain break through. It is a short and direct ascent heading south-east until the OS trig point is reached beside a massive and well built ancient cairn of quartzite blocks. Far away to the east, neatly framed between the summits of Fan Hir and the more distant

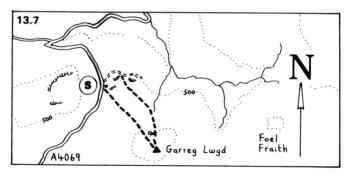

Fan Gyhirych, can be seen the twin summits of Pen y Fan and Corn Du. To the south-west the line of silver on the horizon is Carmarthen Bay and the Bristol Channel.

As a slight variation on the descent, go north passing a peaty pool and follow the tiny outflow stream until the ground steepens. Now go north-west, across an area of shake holes, to the prominent cairn on Foel Fawr and then descend the steep slopes beyond to the disused quarries and the car park.

DELETED TOPS

Enthusiastic peak-baggers may be interested in why some 2000ft tops didn't make it into our list. The following table therefore gives the reason for each exclusion. In some cases it has been possible to prove the matter by reference to the latest OS 1:10,000 maps, either because no separate contour ring is present (and hence the maximum difference between top and col is less than 10m), or because spot heights are given for both top and col which show a difference of less than 15m. Where no spot height was available and where even with on the spot inspection we were in any doubt, we have carried out surveys using a method recommended to us by the Ordnance Survey. Lack of space prevents listing many dozens of other minor tops rejected.

Name of Top	Sheet Ref.	Separation	Reason
Mynydd Pencoed	124-704117 SH	12m	top 766 col 754
Craig Lwyd	124-714118 SH	<10m	no ring contour
Mynydd Gwerngraig	124-736136 SH	9m	estimated
Rhos	125-125323 SJ	<10m	no ring contour
Bryn Gwyn	125-043295 SJ	14m	top 643 col 629
Cefn Gwyntog	125-975275 SH		At 600m too low (new top to south)
Moel Poethion	125-083307 SJ	6m	top 682 col 676
Moel Llechwedd	125-829372 SH	<10m	no ring contour
Pen-aran	125-868247 SH	9m	surveyed
Carreg y Diocyn	125-831363 SH	14m	surveyed
Pen y Cerrig Duon	125-952281 SH	12m	surveyed
Great Creigiau	148-198637 SO	11m	top 646 col 635
Duwynt	160-005206 SO	9m	top 824 col 815
Hay Bluff	161-244366 SO	11m	surveyed
Pen-y-Garn Fawr	161-278311 SO	12m	surveyed
Pumlumon Cwmbiga	135-830899 SN	12.2m	surveyed
Gwaun Cerrig Llwydion	160-041196 SO	14.2m	surveyed
Cadair Bronwen			
North-east Top	125-087352	<15m	surveyed

See www.nuttalls.com for more information.

ALPHABETICAL INDEX OF TOPS

Name of Top	Height metres	Sheet-grid ref.	Walk number	Date of ascent
Allt-fawr	698m	115-682475 SH	5.2	
Allt Lwyd	654m	160-079189 SO	13.2	
Aran Benllyn	885m	125-867243 SH	8.1	
Aran Fawddwy	905m	125-863224 SH	8.1	
Arenig Fach	689m	124-820416 SH	6.2	
Arenig Fawr	854m	124-827370 SH	6.1	
Arenig Fawr South Ridge Top	712m	124-827360 SH	6.1	
Arenig Fawr South Top	836m	124-827366 SH	6.1	
Bache Hill	610m	148-214636 SO	11.4	
Bera Bach	807m	115-672677 SH	1.2	
Bera Mawr	794m	115-675683 SH	1.2	
Black Mixen	650m	148-196644 SO	11.4	
Black Mountain	703m	161-255354 SO	12.1	
Black Mountain South Top	637m	161-267322 SO	12.1	
Bwlch y Ddwyallt	754m	160-055203 SO	13.2	
Cadair Berwyn	827m	125-072327 SJ	7.2	
Cadair Berwyn New Top	830m	125-072324 SJ	7.2	
Cadair Bronwen	785m	125-077346 SJ	7.1	
Cadair Idris	893m	124-711130 SH	10.1	
Carnedd Dafydd	1044m	115-663630 SH	1.1	
Carnedd Llechwedd-llyfn	643m	124-858445 SH	6.2	
Carnedd Llewelyn	1064m	115-684645 SH	1.1	
Carnedd y Ddelw	688m	115-708705 SH	1.3	
Carnedd y Filiast (Arenigs)	669m	124-871446 SH	6.2	
Carnedd y Filiast (Glyders)	821m	115-620628 SH	2.2	
Carnedd y Filiast North Top	721m	115-617631 SH	2.2	
Castell y Gwynt	972m	115-654581 SH	2.1	
Cefn Gwyntog	615m	125-976266 SH	7.5	
Cefn yr Ystrad	617m	160-087137 SO	13.3	
Chwarel y Fan	679m	161-259293 SO	12.1	
Cnicht	689m	115-645466 SH	5.3	
Cnicht North Top	686m	115-648469 SH	5.3	
Corn Du	873m	160-007213 SO	13.1	

Name of Top	Height metres	Sheet-grid ref.	Walk number	Date of ascent
Craig Cerrig-gleisiad	629m	160-961218 SN	13.4	
Craig Cwm Amarch	791m	124-711121 SH	10.1	
Craig Cwm Silyn	734m	115-525503 SH	4.2	
Craig Eigiau	735m	115-713654 SH	1.4	
Craiglwyn	623m	115-731609 SH	1.4	
Craig-y-llyn	622m	124-666120 SH	10.2	
Craigysgafn	689m	124-660443 SH	5.3	
Creigiau Gleision	678m	115-729615 SH	1.4	
Creigiau Gleision North Top	634m	115-734622 SH	1.4	
Crib Goch	923m	115-624552 SH	3.1	
Cribin Fawr	659m	124-795153 SH	10.3	
Crib y Ddysgl	1065m	115-611552 SH	3.1	
Cribyn	795m	160-023213 SO	13.1	
Criby-y-rhiw	670m	124-664248 SH	9.1	
Cyfrwy	811m	124-704134 SH	10.1	
Cyrniau Nod	667m	125-989279 SH	7.5	
Dduallt	662m	124-810274 SH	6.3	
Diffwys	750m	124-661234 SH	9.1	
Diffwys West Top	642m	124-648229 SH	9.1	
Drosgl	758m	115-664680 SH	1.2	
Drum	770m	115-708696 SH	1.3	
Drygarn Fawr	641m	147-862584 SN	11.3	
Elidir Fawr	924m	115-612613 SH	2.2	
Erw y Ddafad-ddu	872m	125-865234 SH	8.1	
Esgeiriau Gwynion	671m	125-890236 SH	8.2	
Fan Brycheiniog	802m	160-825218 SN	13.6	
Fan Fawr	734m	160-970193 SN	13.4	
Fan Fraith	668m	160-887183 SN	13.5	
Fan Frynych	629m	160-958228 SN	13.4	
Fan Gyhirych	725m	160-880190 SN	13.5	
Fan Hir	761m	160-831209 SN	13.6	
Fan Llia	632m	160-938186 SN	13.5	
Fan Nedd	663m	160-913184 SN	13.5	
Fan y Big	719m	160-037207 SO	13.1	
Foel Boeth	616m	124-779342 SH	6.1	

Name of Top	Height metres	Sheet-grid ref.	Walk number	Date of ascent
Foel Cwm Sian Llŵyd	648m	125-996314 SH	7.4	
Foel-fras	942m	115-696682 SH	1.2	
Foel-goch (Glyders)	831m	115-629612 SH	2.2	
Foel Goch (Berwyns)	613m	125-943291 SH	7.5	
Foel Goch (Arenigs)	611m	125-954423 SH	6.4	
Foel Grach	976m	115-689659 SH	1.2	
Foel Gron	629m	115-560569 SH	3.2	
Foel Hafod-fynydd	689m	125-877227 SH	8.2	
Foel Meirch	800m	115-659637 SH	1.1	
Foel Penolau	614m	124-662348 SH	9.2	
Foel Rhudd	659m	125-896240 SH	8.2	
Foel Wen	691m	125-099334 SJ	7.2	
Foel Wen South Top	687m	125-103330 SJ	7.2	
Foel y Geifr	626m	125-937275 SH	7.5	
Gallt y Daren	619m	124-778345 SH	6.1	
Gallt yr Ogof	763m	115-685586 SH	2.3	
Gallt y Wenallt	619m	115-642533 SH	3.1	
Garnedd-goch	700m	115-511495 SH	4.2	
Garnedd Uchaf	926m	115-687669 SH	1.2	
Garreg Las	635m	160-777203 SN	13.6	
Garreg Lwyd	616m	160-740179 SN	13.7	
Gau Graig	683m	124-744141 SH	10.1	
Glasgwm	780m	125-837195 SH	8.3	
Glyder Fach	994m	115-656583 SH	2.1	
Glyder Fawr	999m	115-642580 SH	2.1	
Godor	679m	125-095307 SJ	7.2	
Godor North Top	675m	125-089311 SJ	7.2	
Gorllwyn	613m	147-918591 SN	11.3	
Great Rhos	660m	148-182639 SO	11.4	
Gwaun Lydan	632m	125-880212 SH	8.1	
Gwaun y Llwyni	685m	125-857205 SH	8.1	
Gyrn Wigau	643m	115-654675 SH	1.2	
Llechog	718m	115-606568 SH	3.2	
Llechwedd Du	614m	125-894224 SH	8.2	
Lliwedd Bach	818m	115-628532 SH	3.1	

Name of Top	Height metres	Sheet-grid ref.	Walk number	Date of ascent
Llwytmor	849m	115-689693 SH	1.2	
Maesglase	676m	124-817150 SH	10.3	
Manod Mawr	661m	124-724447 SH	5.4	
Manod Mawr North Top	658m	115-728458 SH	5.4	
Moel Cynghorion	674m	115-587564 SH	3.2	
Moel Druman	676m	115-672476 SH	5.2	
Moel Eilio	726m	115-556577 SH	3.2	
Moel Fferna	630m	125-117398 SJ	7.1	
Moel Hebog	783m	115-565469 SH	4.1	
Moel Lefn	638m	115-553485 SH	4.1	
Moel Llyfnant	751m	124-808351 SH	6.1	
Moel Penamnen	620m	115-717483 SH	5.4	
Meol Siabod	872m	115-705546 SH	5.1	
Moel Sych	827m	125-066318 SJ	7.2	
Moel y Cerrig Duon	625m	125-923241 SH	8.2	
Moel yr Ewig	695m	125-081318 SJ	7.2	
Moel-yr-hydd	648m	115-672454 SH	5.3	
Moel yr Ogof	655m	115-556479 SH	4.1	
Moel Ysgyfarnogod	623m	124-658346 SH	9.2	
Moelwyn Bach	710m	124-660437 SH	5.3	
Moelwyn Mawr	770m	124-658449 SH	5.3	
Moelwyn Mawr North Ridge Top	646m	115-661453 SH	5.3	
Mynydd Graig Goch	610m	115-497485 SH	4.2	
Mynydd Drws-y-coed	695m	115-549518 SH	4.2	
Mynydd Llysiau	663m	161-208279 SO	12.2	
Mynydd Mawr	698m	115-540547 SH	4.3	
Mynydd Moel	863m	124-728137 SH	10.1	
Mynydd Perfedd	812m	115-623619 SH	2.2	
Mynydd Tal-y-mignedd	653m	115-535514 SH	4.2	
Mynydd Tarw	681m	125-113324 SJ	7.2	
Pen Allt-mawr	719m	161-207243 SO	12.2	
Pen Bwlch Llandrillo Top	621m	125-090369 SJ	7.1	
Pen Cerrig-calch	701m	161-217224 SO	12.2	
Pen Llithrig-y-wrâch	799m	115-716623 SH	1.4	

Name of Top	Height metres	Sheet-grid ref.	Walk number	Date of ascent
Waun Garnedd-y-filiast	650m	124-874452 SH	6.2	
Waun Lefrith	677m	160-798215 SN	13.6	
Waun-oer	670m	124-786148 SH	10.3	
Waun Rydd	769m	160-062206 SO	13.2	
Y Foel Goch	805m	115-678582 SH	2.3	
Y Garn (Rhinogs)	629m	124-703230 SH	9.3	
Y Garn (Pumlumon)	684m	135-776852 SN	11.1	
Y Garn (Moel Hebog)	633m	115-551526 SH	4.2	
Y Garn (Glyders)	947m	115-631596 SH	2.2	
Y Groes Fagl	659m	125-988290 SH	7.5	
Y Gyrn	619m	160-989216 SN	13.4	
Y Llethr	756m	124-661258 SH	9.1	
Y Lliwedd	898m	115-622533 SH	3.1	
Y Lliwedd East Peak	893m	115-624533 SH	3.1	
Yr Aran	747m	115-604515 SH	3.3	
Yr Elen	962m	115-674651 SH	1.1	
Ysgafell Wen	672m	115-667481 SH	5.2	
Ysgafell Wen Far North Top	650m	115-664488 SH	5.2	
Ysgafell Wen North Top	669m	115-664486 SH	5.2	

NEW TOPS (since Edition 1) - see above for details

Carnedd y Filiast North Top

Castell y Gwynt

Cnicht North Top

Craiglwyn

Foel Meirch

Moelwyn Mawr North Ridge Top

Mynydd Graig Goch

Waun Camddwr

Waun Garnedd-y-filiast

Waun Lefrith

Maesglase - the summit has moved west to Craig Rhiw-erch.